Praise for *The Forever Transaction*

The future belongs to businesses who transform their interactions with customers from mere transactions to meaningful engagements that create long-term fans. Robbie Baxter is an expert guide to this powerful business model. Read this book and start transforming your business now!

> **Chris Capossela**, Chief Marketing Officer and
> Executive Vice President, Microsoft

Robbie's work is an essential blueprint for any company or organization looking to build strong and lasting relationships with their customers.

> **Mike Argon**, Senior Vice President of Content, Twitch

Subscriptions are all the rage these days, but to stand out and truly capitalize on their potential a business must start and end with a solid understanding of its customers. Baxter's excellent book shows you exactly how to do this, with fresh case studies and practical tools that spell out what it really takes to ensure that "forever" is just that.

> **Marco Bertini**, Professor of Marketing, ESADE Business
> School of Barcelona, Spain

When customers become community members, business is transformed. *The Forever Transaction* offers an insider's perspective for making this shift in all kinds of organizations. This is the future of business, but you can get there today.

> **Gina Bianchini,** Founder and Chief Executive Officer,
> Mighty Networks

In the world of SaaS, subscription pricing is just the beginning. Baxter shares the secrets of how you keep your business model current and relevant for your subscribers. Baxter is a guru on subscription and membership models. She shares her pro tips and her passion here about how to steer your business to the future.

> **Zac Bookman**, Chief Executive Officer, OpenGov

Kudos to Baxter for another home-run book. She has a flair for breaking down complex business concepts into bite-size chunks. She shares real-world examples that de-mystify the technical aspects of membership-building, making it accessible to anyone. Whether you lead a company, association, or nonprofit, this book is a must read if you want to thrive—not just survive—in today's Membership Economy.

> **Leslie Crutchfield**, Executive Director of Business for Impact at Georgetown University's McDonough School of Business and bestselling author of *How Change Happens*

The Forever Transaction is an essential read for any business seeking to leverage the power of subscriptions to engage and retain customers.

> **Nir Eyal**, bestselling author of *Hooked* and *Indistractable*

The growing excitement for subscription-based business models is matched by the danger that poorly managed programs (and expectations) can be their downfall. Executives need clear advice backed by years of world-class experience in this domain, and no one can bring it better than Robbie Kellman Baxter. *The Forever Transaction* is the best, most indispensable set of best practices I've ever seen on building and sustaining a subscription-based business model.

> **Peter S. Fader**, Frances and Pei-Yuan Chia Professor of Marketing at The Wharton School of the University of Pennsylvania and bestselling author of *Customer Centricity* and *The Customer Centricity Playbook*

The rise of the cloud and mobile technologies, combined with the declining cost of storage, has led to new competitors in every industry. Choosing the right metrics makes all the difference and retention is now one of the most important. Robbie can show you how to establish a forever transaction with your customers.

> **Sarah Friar**, Chief Executive Officer, Nextdoor, and Board Director of Walmart and Slack

Member-centricity is the core of successful associations and, increasingly, thriving companies. In *The Forever Transaction*, Robbie Baxter captures the techniques that Amazon, Netflix, LinkedIn, and others are using to build sustained customer relationships. Leaders of any membership organization can gain insight and practical tips from Robbie Baxter's book.

> **John H. Graham IV**, FASAE, CAE, Chief Executive Officer and President, American Society of Association Executives (ASAE)

Read this book alongside *The Membership Economy* to discover the magic ingredients of long-term membership success.

> **Tom Greene**, Chief Operating Officer, Wizarding World Digital, Official Hub for Harry Potter and Fantastic Beasts

Robbie's first book, *The Membership Economy*, became my company's North Star as we made the transition to a membership model. The guidance she provides in *The Forever Transaction* is equally as compelling, even visionary. If you're creating or running a subscription business, this is a great road map.

> **McKeel Hagerty**, Chief Executive Officer, Hagerty Group, and Global Board Chairman Emeritus, YPO

Subscription models are disrupting nearly every industry—don't be left behind. Robbie Baxter is the expert on how to start, scale, and sustain forever transactions. *The Forever Transaction* provides the soup-to-nuts—and secret sauce—guide on how to attract and keep the best customers by tailoring a value-laden offering that meets their need while growing your business.

> **Whitney Johnson**, bestselling author of *Disrupt Yourself* and *Build an A Team*

Recurring revenue is the holy grail, and Robbie Baxter is giving us the map to find it. Building on 15 years of experience in Silicon Valley and beyond, Baxter provides fresh case studies and practical tools to disruption-proof your organization.

> **Charlene Li**, Founder and Senior Fellow at Altimeter, a Prophet company and bestselling author of *The Disruption Mindset*

Baxter offers clear and actionable advice with a global perspective for any organization looking to improve customer lifetime value and grow a sustainable subscription business.

Philip Lindqvist, Chief Strategy Officer and Head of Distribution, Bonnier Broadcasting

If you're looking for a blueprint on how to succeed in the membership economy, this is it. Robbie Baxter has extensive knowledge of the subscription business model, and fortunately for entrepreneurs everywhere, she put it in writing.

Nick Mehta, Chief Executive Officer, Gainsight

Robbie has built a powerful practical guidebook to help companies thrive in the membership world. *The Forever Transaction* provides a framework to help transform your business, building customer loyalty and revenues for a lifetime. Masterfully done!

Rajesh Ram, Cofounder and Chief Customer Officer, Egnyte

In this book, growth strategist Robbie Kellman Baxter teaches the most important business strategy of our time: creating enduring relationships with customers. Through accessible research and practical guides, *The Forever Transaction* takes the mystery out of what it takes to create a forever organization.

Lisa Kay Solomon, Designer in Residence at the Stanford d.School and bestselling coauthor of *Moments of Impact* and *Design a Better Business*

Companies that sell products to strangers aren't going to last long in this new subscription economy. This is an excellent playbook for any organization looking to launch a sustainable membership strategy.

Tien Tzuo, Founder and Chief Executive Officer, Zuora, and bestselling author of *Subscribed*

THE
FOREVER
TRANSACTION

How to Build a Subscription Model So Compelling, Your Customers Will Never Want to Leave

ROBBIE KELLMAN BAXTER

New York   Chicago   San Francisco   Athens   London   Madrid
Mexico City   Milan   New Delhi   Singapore   Sydney   Toronto

1 2 3 4 5 6 7 8 9   LCR   25 24 23 22 21 20

ISBN: 978-1-260-45870-1
MHID: 1-260-45870-9

e-ISBN: 978-1-260-45871-8
e-MHID: 1-260-45871-7

This publication is designed to provide accurate and authoritative information in regard to the subject matter covered. It is sold with the understanding that neither the author nor the publisher is engaged in rendering legal, accounting, securities trading, or other professional services. If legal advice or other expert assistance is required, the services of a competent professional person should be sought.
    —*From a Declaration of Principles Jointly Adopted by a Committee of the American Bar Association and a Committee of Publishers and Associations*

McGraw-Hill Education books are available at special quantity discounts to use as premiums and sales promotions or for use in corporate training programs. To contact a representative, please visit the Contact Us pages at www.mhprofessional.com.

To Molly, Annabel, Nate, and especially to Bob,
my own forever transaction

CONTENTS

INTRODUCTION:
THE WHY OF FOREVER

I just ordered a new electric toothbrush.

We Kellmans are prolific plaque producers, so I usually go for the most expensive one, with all the bells and whistles. When I saw that the Oral-B Pro 6000 has Bluetooth and is "smart," I was hooked. In addition to buzzing every 30 seconds to move me to the next quadrant, the Pro 6000 has a mobile app that tracks where, how much, and how hard I brush. There are different programs to achieve specific goals, like whitening teeth or caring for gums. There's a camera feature I haven't figured out yet, but I'm guessing it allows communication with the "experts" at Oral-B who can give feedback on how I'm doing, when I need a new brush head, and what additional products might help (floss, mouthwash, toothpaste, special brushes—who knew there were so many options!).

I get a free toothbrush from my dentist each visit, but instead of settling for that, I spent 100 bucks. I'm sending Oral-B information about how frequently I brush, how often I change brush heads, and what "challenges" bother me most. I'm giving them permission to reach out to me via email and directly through an app I'm using, ideally twice a day.

Instead of going through a retailer like Amazon or CVS, Oral-B now has a direct line to me. I'm considering subscribing to all my oral hygiene products from them, instead of purchasing through an intermediary. For years, I've wanted someone to make a "forever promise" to keep my teeth and gums healthy. Because of the way they're delivering on my desired outcome, I'm becoming a member of the Oral-B family. And Oral-B is becoming part of the Membership Economy.

The Membership Economy is my name for the massive trend among organizations to tap into the value of long-term, formal relationships through subscriptions. It means moving from an ownership model to one of access, from a single payment to multiple recurring payments, from an anonymous transaction to a known relationship, and from one-way—or even two-way—communication to a full community gathered under the umbrella of the organization.

Many of these new Membership Economy organizations employ tactics like subscription pricing, premium loyalty clubs, and mobile apps, but the unifying attribute of Membership Economy organizations is the establishment of a forever transaction with the people they serve. Organizations treat customers like members. And customers trust that the organization will continue to evolve products and services to deliver on that forever promise. As a result, customers stop considering alternatives to achieve their goals.

In your personal life as a consumer, you might have a forever transaction with a company like Microsoft, when you use Office 365, or Unilver, when you join their Dollar Shave Club. Or you might have a forever transaction with a trusted subject matter expert like Dave Ramsey, or with a nonprofit like AARP or a megachurch. A forever transaction, as the outgrowth of a forever promise of value, can bring virtually any kind of organization into the Membership Economy. You know what these relationships feel like as a consumer or participant. How can you re-create this experience for your organization?

In my first book, *The Membership Economy*, I explained why organizations were moving to this new model. I wanted to demonstrate—even *prove*—that a massive transformational trend was underway. People initially doubted the broad-based applicability of subscription pricing, customer-centricity, and community. At the time, executives and entrepreneurs kept saying—"Robbie, what you're doing is interesting, but that's not really relevant to me." They would latch onto a single business without seeing the pattern: "We're not Netflix" or "We're an association, not a tech startup" or "But our industry (healthcare/financial services/cable/nonprofit) is different."

Much has changed since then. Companies now want forever transactions. They actively seek recurring, predictable revenue. Often, this revenue comes in the form of a subscription. The average American pays $237 a month for subscription services, such as video streaming, newspapers, software, and meal kits, according to a July 2018 report from West Monroe Partners. This is becoming typical around the world, with Asia and Europe leading growth in subscription expenditures. A November 2018 survey from The Harris Poll and subscription-based services platform Zuora asked consumers whether they thought they'd be using more subscription services in two years; 53 percent of Chinese people surveyed said yes, as did 42 percent in Spain and 40 percent in Italy.[1]

Subscriptions aren't the only path to the Membership Economy. Some organizations offer a free membership, or a premium membership that gives access to a bundle of services, or a points system tracking and rewarding engagement. The common denominator, whatever tactics are used, is that Membership Economy organizations assume they're going to deal with the same customers, forever. The well-being of the customer, and the health of the long-term relationship, is the highest aim of these organizations. Because, if you want forever, you have to be trustworthy. You have to keep your promise.

Today, people understand my elevator pitch. Readers all over the world have purchased *The Membership Economy*. I have advised dozens of organizations on five continents on building forever transactions. I've keynoted and consulted with news publishers, car wash executives, software entrepreneurs, business owners, association CEOs, hospitalists, entrepreneurs, executives, and investors in almost any industry you could imagine. Now people come to me with specific questions relating to their business, no longer asking about the *why* but the *how*. They see the important pieces but are unsure how to fit them all together. This is good for my consulting and speaking business. But I can't help everyone directly, which is why I'm writing this book.

For this book, I've looked for the "how" patterns and unpacked what I do with my clients. *The Membership Economy* described what I was noticing. *The Forever Transaction* shares specifics about what I'm doing with my clients so you can transform your organization as well.

What Is a Forever Transaction?

I first hit upon the idea of a forever transaction soon after I subscribed to Netflix in 2001. I remember the timing because those red envelopes in my mailbox were a lifesaver when I was up most nights with my newborn and/or my toddler. I wrote in *The Membership Economy*, "Unlike the rental stores that depended on each transaction to drive revenue, Netflix started out in the early days with just one 'forever transaction'—after you sign up and until you cancel, you get the same great experience without having to enter your payment information ever again."[2]

I want to show you how to create your own forever transaction. It's about orchestrating the moment when customers remove their "consumer hats" and don "member hats," commit to your organization for the long term, and *stop considering alternatives*. For many companies this is the holy grail: loyal recurring customers, often paying automatically, indefinitely.

To earn a "forever transaction" you must offer a "forever promise" in return. You commit to deliver a result, solve a pain point, or achieve an outcome for your members forever, in exchange for their loyalty.

To justify the forever transaction, you need to rethink not just your pricing, but all the elements through which you deliver value. That's the idea at the heart of this book.

How to Read this Book

Some of my early readers confessed that they were taking action and not finishing the reading. They were applying principles to their businesses as they read. That's OK—great even! I want to spur you to action. My dearest wish is that this book becomes marked up and dirty, due to frequent use, no matter which parts you use, even if you never reach the conclusion.

The book is divided into three parts and a total of 19 chapters. Each chapter and part can stand alone. Read the book from start to finish like a prix fixe meal, snack on a single part, or go à la carte as your needs require. My goal is to aid comprehension and inspire action.

Part One: Launch, will help you assess where you are and where you need to invest early on. These chapters are designed to ground you in membership. I don't delve as deeply into the "what and why" as I did in *The Membership Economy*, but I do hit the high points. For deeper understanding, read *The Membership Economy*.

This first part will provide ideas for launching an initial test and conducting basic research to ascertain your potential for joining the Membership Economy. Whether you're just getting started, or you've experimented, or you're trying to reinvent your subscription or membership model with the latest techniques, this part can help you be certain the fundamentals are soundly in place.

Part Two: Scale, helps you build on small successes to create a full-scale forever transaction. It addresses the foundational systems and processes your organization will need for rapid business growth. After reading, you will be able to nurture an organizational culture that supports a forever transaction, accelerate growth through acquisition and iteration, anticipate common setbacks and correct mistakes, build the right infrastructure, price strategically, and track the right metrics.

Part Three: Lead, contains chapters to ensure that your model evolves to remain relevant and valuable to the people you serve. I break out some of the challenges mature Membership Economy businesses face: focusing too much on an aging cohort, getting distracted by short-term goals, going global, and dealing with subscription fatigue. Because I'm always asked what the future holds, I also include a chapter touching on some intriguing trends on the horizon.

I Wrote This Book for You

The size and age of your organization doesn't matter. Neither does your industry or your title. Whether you're an investor, entrepreneur, executive, or individual contributor, if you face competition and need sales and marketing strength to attract, engage, and retain customers, you can benefit from this book.

A Word About *The Membership Economy* and *The Forever Transaction*

The Forever Transaction is designed to teach you how to be successful in the world I described in *The Membership Economy*. The two books are substantially different, with little overlap. I've included a glossary to help with key terms and ideas.

If you want to understand the Membership Economy on a macro level, read the first book. To implement these principles in your organization and build better, more valuable and enduring relationships with the people you serve, read this one. You have a forever transaction when people say things like "I don't even care exactly what I'm paying because this organization solves my problems and helps me achieve my goals. It's like they know exactly what I need. I trust them."

Most organizations that thrive in the Membership Economy use subscription pricing, but not all. These organizations share other attributes as well, such as a strong and well-defined onboarding process, metrics that value engagement and customer lifetime value as much as acquisition, and a digital component that connects the customer directly with the organization, and often with other members.

I want to help you build forever transactions with the people you serve in a way that drives value for them and for you. It goes beyond making money, although using this model is profitable. You must care deeply about the customer. Your product has to be designed to produce the best results for your best customers—in a way that earns their trust, forever.

PART ONE Launch

You might be intrigued by the concept of membership, of bypassing intermediaries to take your services directly to customers. Maybe you have a loyalty program but it's not engaging your most profitable prospects and customers. You need to modernize with a model attractive to a new audience and/or one that increases the frequency and duration of visits by existing customers. If you're launching a new business model or if you want to make sure your fundamentals are strong, this part is for you.

Are you an entrepreneur with an idea and a bit of angel funding? Nonprofit? Fortune 500 executive wanting to drive recurring revenue without cannibalizing existing business? Somewhere between? If so, start here.

These first seven chapters will ground you, identifying where and how to begin your journey in building a forever transaction with your customers.

Chapter 1: Welcome to the World of Forever

Chapter 2: Are You Ready for Forever?

Chapter 3: Forever Begins with a Plan

Chapter 4: Define Your Forever Promise

Chapter 5: Choose the Right Who for the How

Chapter 6: Develop Your First Experiments

Chapter 7: Test, Learn, Adjust

---

1 Welcome to the World of Forever

Subscriptions and memberships seem to be everywhere. It's easy to see why. They drive "forever transactions," those incredibly valuable customer relationships in which people sign up once but pay again and again, often without considering alternatives. Subscription pricing structures can increase customer lifetime value (CLV), drive predictable recurring revenue, and generate monster valuations. They can also provide behavioral data that keeps you close to the customer and can be a defense against disruption. And a membership mindset focuses your organization on the long-term needs of your customers and creates all kinds of ways to layer in value. But the journey to forever isn't simple, and there's no single right way to do it. As you make the shift to treating customers like members, you have to make many decisions, some of which feel risky.

For example, Apple lets you either "rent" a movie for a 24-hour viewing or buy it for a fixed price and watch it repeatedly. In 2019, Apple announced a Netflix-like model, Apple TV+, with a monthly "all you can eat" charge. Many believe the company's success hinges on a move to subscription services and away from hardware.[1] Adding a membership component generates a million questions for any company building a forever transaction: whether to charge more for the most popular titles, what to do with preexisting pricing models, and how to ensure that the portfolio of options is user-friendly. It's never as simple as just setting an affordable subscription price, but it can be critical to your business's long-term success.

> ∞
>
> **In order to find the right "forever" for the people you serve, you first have to closely investigate your organization, your objectives, and your customers.**

You're probably reading this book because you like the idea of a forever transaction. You want to figure out how to repackage your value as a subscription in a way that's so attractive that customers commit to recurring payment. You also need to learn how to continually adjust what you offer based on customer feedback and changes in the broader environment to continue to justify their loyalty. In order to find the right "forever" for the people you serve, you first have to closely investigate your organization, your objectives, and your customers. We're going to do that in this chapter and the next. I'm not going to sugarcoat it—doing a serious self-assessment takes time and is strenuous. But—I promise you—it's worth it. If you can build a successful model that wins your customers' loyalty for the long term and justifies automated recurring payments, you will have a more predictable cash flow, better customer data, and most likely, a higher valuation from your investors.

I've worked with organizations of all types and sizes that ran into trouble when trying to achieve the forever transaction because of unrecognized internal constraints:

- A content streaming company had moderate success experimenting with subscription pricing. But the transition team lacked permission to lose any money as they expanded the program. Nor could they dictate necessary changes to the product team or sales channels as they moved to sell directly to consumers.

- A beauty company had a large loyalty membership program, ostensibly to build a "forever transaction" without subscription pricing—a good idea. However, even though every customer joined, the program didn't drive behavioral changes. Salespeople often paid the fee themselves to close the deal because they couldn't persuade customers of the value and because the membership fee was smaller than the commission. As a result the "members" weren't aware of the benefits of membership and were unlikely to renew.
- The leaders of a nonprofit organization thought they were fully engaged in the Membership Economy, but they treated membership like another of many products to purchase such as trainings, conferences, and bumper stickers. They took pride in their mission, but they were financially focused, not member-centric; as a result, they were losing members.

Different companies, different issues. The content streaming company lacked leadership support and understanding about what it would take to transform. The beauty company needed to realign its present program with the goals of consumers and the company. The nonprofit needed to revisit its ideal new member and member journey to devise an offering that would better engage members. In each case, it was important not to jump to the solution before analyzing the problem and the objective. That's what this chapter is designed to help you do.

Assessing Specifics for the Business Model

Company leaders often tell me "we want to be the Netflix of our industry." This stimulates a revealing discussion. I usually ask each team member what that would mean for their organization. It's amazing how different people interpret "being like Netflix."

For some, being like Netflix means simple subscription pricing on a monthly cadence. For others, it means offering access to a catalog in contrast to ownership of specific titles. Still others laser in on creating

> The most successful organizations begin by asking what membership could mean for their customers and then ask what membership could mean for the organization.

unique content or having a multiplatform strategy.

The most successful organizations begin by asking what membership could mean for their customers and then ask what membership could mean for the organization. After they've framed the value they're trying to create, *then* they dig into specifics around functionality, pricing, and service.

Size Doesn't Matter

I have worked with some of the world's largest organizations, and with entrepreneurs just starting out. The same principles apply all along the spectrum. A nail salon with longtime loyal customers making regular weekly visits can easily transition to a membership model offering "perfect nails" as a forever promise and incorporating chipped nail fixes into pricing. A mechanic can provide regular house calls to ensure that the car is well maintained and address problems preemptively.

> If you have a business *of any size* that depends on sales and marketing to attract and retain customers, this book can help you bring it into the Membership Economy.

A solopreneur like John Lee Dumas of the award-winning podcast Entrepreneurs on Fire and podcaster community Podcasters' Paradise, builds a forever transaction around his subject matter expertise of building podcasts as a solopreneur. One of the world's most successful daily podcasters for business builders, Dumas earns eight figures through podcast sponsorships, courses on creating podcasts, and coaching and mastermind offerings.

If you have a business *of any size* that depends on sales and marketing to attract and retain customers, this book can help you bring it into the Membership Economy.

Transformation for Membership Natives

Even organizations that launch with membership pricing struggle to be fully member-centric. Many establish a forever promise with subscription pricing but fail to continue to optimize the product for "forever." Organizations starting from scratch with subscription and what they think is a membership mindset might still have departments focused on individual transactions rather than ongoing relationships, which will create headwinds.

Consider a streaming media company that offers monthly pricing for a catalog of content that can be consumed in one month. The company separated the acquisition and retention teams. The acquisition team designed a marketing campaign for the subscription focused on an exclusive title—a national sports championship—generating many sign-ups right before the championship and many cancellations immediately after it. The retention team was then blamed for this easily anticipated churn. Acquisition and retention teams need to understand cause and effect and share some metrics.

Growing organizations often architect customized options in response to customer requests. Sometimes this customization doesn't produce a better customer experience. Imagine going to the doctor and saying, "I have a headache; I'd like some brain surgery, please" or "I'd like brain surgery, but I don't need follow-up visits." Individual customers shouldn't dictate your pricing and packaging of value. Customers can share their pain points, the "symptoms" of their problem, but you must supply the diagnoses and prescriptions.

As pure membership businesses grow, they may acquire outliers that may not align with the company's overall direction. For example, some purchasers of Peloton bikes—among the priciest of stationary bikes because of their built-in tablet devices and video classes—only want to use the tablet to watch TV. If Peloton listened to those customers, it might produce a copycat bike *not* differentiated with streaming content. Instead, it remains focused on *members* desiring the most interactive, motivational community experience available in home fitness. If you just want to watch TV while you ride, don't buy a Peloton. I'm pretty sure the Peloton sales people would say the same thing.

You have to be willing to risk "pruning" some of your customers if they aren't interested in the problem you're solving.

Obviously, your successful implementation of the forever transaction is going to depend on your ability to accurately understand both your internal challenges and external capacities. More than that, you are going to need a laser-like focus on defining and attracting the right customers. Don't worry. I can help with this: that's where we're going to start in this book.

There are as many ways to design a forever transaction as there are organizations. The devil is in the details as you determine what your organization's model should be.

What to Do Next

Before reading the next chapter, answer the following questions:

1. Are you just getting started with a forever transaction?
2. How far along do you think you are?

Write an honest answer—you don't have to show it to anyone else! Then, read Chapter 2 to learn the questions that I would ask if I were there to help you. Use the assessments in Chapter 2 to measure your organization's readiness or maturity to develop a forever transaction.

2 Are You Ready for Forever?

If I were advising your organization, I would start by asking many questions to assess where you are now. I would want to understand what you're doing well and where there are gaps.

First, I'd ascertain how close you are to being a Membership Economy company right now. Do you have any kind of subscription offering? Do you have anything labeled a membership? Or a loyalty program? These are obvious starting points, but pricing a subscription or having an offering called a membership doesn't mean you are thoughtfully nurturing long-term relationships with the people you serve or maximizing customer lifetime value (CLV):

1. Do you look like a Membership Economy company with subscriptions and/or memberships?
2. Are you customer-centric? Really?
3. Do you have a strong and flexible tech infrastructure and team?

Next we'd discuss business culture: do you love your customers and treat them well? This is essential in the expectation of a long-term relationship. What's the mindset of the CEO and board? Are they positioned to invest in the long-term health of the business, or are they desperate to hit a quarterly number?

Third, I would investigate your capabilities. How sophisticated is the tech team and the tech stack—the combination of software and hardware they're building on? Old technology implemented to serve a different business model can make it difficult to be nimble even with enhancements. Ironically, startups with no customers or technology at all have an advantage because they start with a clean slate. Even if larger companies have resources to start fresh, they're often reluctant to abandon legacy systems and processes.

I would ask how well you are leveraging technology to learn about your customer. Beyond a certain size, developing long-term known relationships with customers demands a powerful tech infrastructure. Technology implementation is often the biggest gating factor to scaling even the most successful test. Without it, companies can't collect and analyze data, manage interactions consistently, or provide customers with a personalized experience. Digitally native companies have an advantage, even if they're moving from ad-centric to customer-centric or from a traditional e-commerce site to a membership or subscription-based e-tailer. I'd extensively question what your company is trying to accomplish as a foundation for ongoing conversation.

In this chapter, we'll explore these questions to determine where you'll need to focus as you transform your business to one built on a forever transaction.

The Forever Transaction Self-Assessment

Your strategy depends on how your organization is oriented in several dimensions relevant to the forever transaction. It's not enough to implement subscription pricing. In fact, many businesses build strong forever transactions without using subscription pricing at all.

Assess your readiness and potential pitfalls in these areas:

- Leadership support (C-suite champions)
- Team lead
- Ongoing formal customer relationship
- Target customers
- Technology
- Culture

Let's examine each element more closely and break out the diagnostic questions.

Leadership Support: C-Suite Champions

Leaders can't just pay lip service to the strategy. They have to allocate resources and track the right metrics. No factor is more critical to your success. If leadership support is missing in your organization, suggest that the leadership team read this book.

Leadership Support Assessment
- Is leadership (CEO, board) committed to a membership model?
- Is leadership providing the team lead (see below) with staffing, budget, public support and executive sponsorship to assess the opportunity and implement a strategy until it's mature and thriving?
- Does leadership prioritize long-term customer relationships and CLV over quarterly revenue and/or successful product releases?

Many membership models fail because the organization lacks a strategic lead who builds a big picture vision that incorporates the entire organization instead of focusing on operational tasks.

Team Lead

Many membership models fail because the organization lacks a strategic lead who builds a big picture vision that incorporates the entire organization instead of focusing on operational tasks. Sometimes when you do one thing, it impacts your ability to take the next step—one goal depends on another. Someone must foresee those dependencies.

Long-range understanding is rare, but it is a critical strength for the person leading this initiative. A team lead with credibility, seniority, and a strategic orientation is a game changer. (See Chapter 5, "Choose the Right Who for the How," for a detailed discussion.)

Team Lead Assessment

* Does the organization have a designated team lead who has a history with the company, occupies a senior level in the organization, and demonstrates strategic and creative leadership?
* Is the team lead passionate about customer-centricity and membership?
* Does the team lead have sufficient resources (budget, staff, authority) to build the business?

Ongoing Formal Customer Relationship

What's the current status of your customer relationships? Some organizations focus completely on maximizing individual transactions. They worry they might never access this anonymous customer's wallet again. Consequently, they upsell like crazy, even knowing the customer may experience buyer's remorse later. At the other end of the spectrum are pure membership organizations; every member gets the full range of benefits to solve a problem forever. For example, Rick Warren's Saddleback Church provides myriad member pathways to what Warren calls "a purpose-driven life," with multiple campuses, streaming services, small groups for personal connection, books, and more than 200 ministries.

Many organizations fall between these extremes. Software-as-a-service (SaaS) companies often charge customers like member organizations but don't provide the onboarding, support, communications, or product features supportive of ongoing engagement. Many retailers and hospitality companies have points-based "loyalty programs." These offer a reciprocal exchange of discounts and benefits for depth and frequency of purchase, with little emphasis on building an emotional connection. Then, there are customer-centric organizations with transactional pricing, whose customers return again and again and feel a sense of community.

Customer Relationship Assessment

- Does your organization have formal ongoing relationships with your customers?
- Are your products or services sold in a one-time, transactional fashion, as ongoing services, or in a contractual relationship?
- Does your pricing favor loyal and longtime purchasers?
- If you're transactional, are there programs and processes to smooth the gap between transactions, like a loyalty program or community?

Target Customers

Additionally, I use a concept of best customer (best member) to assess readiness. Your best customers are the ones you'd like to replicate and often are your most valuable customers. They pay on time, use your products well, get great value for their investment, and refer others to your organization. And because your products become habits, and are important to them, they are not price sensitive.

Startup organizations can launch with a hypothesis about who their ideal customer will be, but they should evaluate their assumptions as data emerges.

Established organizations can determine who their most profitable and/or happiest customers are. Some organizations leverage this information to optimize products and services. Others only use these insights to target marketing activities. Some don't know much about their customers; they sell through intermediaries (retailers and resellers) or run a cash business with limited data.

Target Customer Assessment
- Do you know your target customers, and, more importantly, who you best serve?
- Do you track your most valuable customers and their purchasing patterns?
- What data do you collect about your customers, whether business to business (B2B) or business to consumer (B2C)?
- Are you harnessing the power of superusers* as ambassadors, feedback sources, or new customer mentors?

Technology

Technology is key to having a forever transaction with the customer. And it requires investment. You can use workarounds in the testing phases, like having a person manually register new members or running your emails outside your Customer Relationship Management (CRM) system, but to scale, you will need to communicate, bill, support, and deliver to your customers in a frequent and flexible manner. You can't scale up with manual processes. You must adapt to changes in hours or days, not months or years. Every person in the organization must be, if not tech-savvy, at least tech-knowledgeable.

Technology Assessment
- Will your technology support a forever transaction?
- How quickly can you alter your product delivery system or run a test on a new segment?

---

* For more on harnessing the power of superusers, see Chapter 6 of *The Membership Economy*, "Onboard Members for Success and Superusers."

- How flexible is your billing system? Is it optimized for membership pricing, trial offers, and easy maneuvering among pricing tiers?
- Do your communication systems engage customers throughout their journey?
- Can members connect with each another? Community can be a key component of a successful forever transaction.
- Can you track the relationship between behavior and CLV?

Culture

Every organization claims to be customer-centric. But organizational structure often reveals the true strategy. You can find clues in the leadership background, even office decor. (What's on the wall? IPO hardware? Old products? Customer photos and letters?) Key companywide metrics also present a window to underlying strategy. Some organizations rally around quarterly earnings, new customers, and major product releases. Others focus on "member-since" milestones, CLV, and net promoter scores.

Cultural Assessment
- How do your employees talk about customers? Are they empathetic? Do they know any of your best customers personally?
- How long has it been since your leadership team was on the front line?
- What grounds your business philosophy? Are you member-centric? Product-centric? Financial-centric?
- Where's the power? (Hint: If it's all with product/sales/finance, you have an issue.)

Diagnosing Yourself

For each of the categories in the table, give yourself a grade of 1 to 3. The more threes you check, the stronger your organization's commitment to a forever promise. Twos mean that you have the necessary infrastructure but may not have a culture that supports this transformation. If you have mostly ones, you may struggle to successfully launch your new model, and you may want to work to build internal alignment before diving in.

TABLE 2.1 Forever Transaction Self-Diagnosis

	1	2	3
Leadership Support for Membership	Leader is quarterly focused	Strong project manager and light support from CEO	CEO's legacy rests on membership mindset
Team Lead	No dedicated lead	Have a dedicated, low-level manager	Senior strategist with tenure
Ongoing, Formal Relationship with Customer	Don't track customers; go through distributor	Track all metrics with CLV as key and/or have great customer relationships	Customer is at the center of everything, and recurring payments prove it
Subscription	No	Testing	Yes
Target Customers	Everyone	Tracking customers by cohort, and willing to narrow the top of the funnel to optimize engagement	Well-defined by behavior and need states as well as demographics or psychographics
Technology	Old and transactional	Ready to invest in tech	Sophisticated stack in place and ready for customization
Culture	Product-centric*	Someone on the team responsible for customer voice	Customer-centric

---

* For more information on the distinction between product-oriented and relationship-oriented businesses, please see Chapter 4 of *The Membership Economy*, "Build the Right Organization."

If you've scored low on all fronts, that's OK. It's also fine if you're just getting started. But it's important to scope the work ahead of you and dedicate the resources to be successful.

Once you've assessed where you are, you can dive into the work. The rest of this book devotes itself to helping you build and sustain a business built around a forever transaction.

What to Do Next

- Assess where you are in the maturity model using the previous table.
- Use the chapters that follow to fill the gaps, as described below:

TABLE 2.2 Forever Transaction Prescriptions

Leadership Support	If you're low on leadership support, show your leadership team Chapter 1, "Welcome to the World of Forever."
Team Lead	Read Chapter 5, "Choose the Right Who for the How," and make sure you have a team lead who has credibility across the organization, the right resources, and the right mindset to build your forever transaction.
Ongoing Formal Relationship with Customers	Read Chapter 3, "Forever Begins with a Plan."
Target Customers	To start mapping your customer journey and understand your "best customer," read Chapter 4, "Define Your Forever Promise."
Technology	See Chapter 11, "Choose the Technology to Scale."
Culture	Pay attention to the strategies in Chapter 8, "Manage Emotions, Transform Culture, and Build a Shared Vision."

3 Forever Begins with a Plan

Defining and committing to a forever promise is a major undertaking. You need to make the business case to justify the effort. Subscription pricing is a potentially powerful tactic, but by itself, it's not a business model. The why and how of implementation matter. The business case is crucial because it forces organizations to articulate goals, identify success metrics, and prepare for the operational implications before diving in and planning their subscription model.

I recommend that you begin by stepping back to define why you want to pursue this strategy and specify what you hope to achieve. What's in it for your customers, and what's in it for you? Answering these questions will help you develop the high-level business case, a necessary step before getting granular with things like pricing and features.

> The business case is crucial because it forces organizations to articulate goals, identify success metrics, and prepare for the operational implications before diving in.

Benefits of Membership
(for the Best Customers)

It's likely you've already been thinking about the benefits you could gain through a more direct, ongoing relationship with your customers. But have you thought about what's in it for them? When your goals align with your members' motivations, you have a powerful and lucrative model that also inspires your employees. Here are some of the goals that attract and retain members:

- Save money
- Save time
- Mitigate risk
- Meet like-minded people
- Get expert advice
- Enjoy more service
- Discover new things
- Access a broader range of choices
- Increase flexibility (make a smaller up-front commitment)
- Access exclusive stuff
- Achieve status and recognition
- Feel part of something, recognized, and/or understood

Benefits of the Forever Transaction
(for the Organization)

There are many ways to deliver on a forever promise, with varied benefits for the organization. Focus on your primary goals, not all of them:

- Identify and nurture leads. People who subscribe to your offering are likely to upgrade.
- Develop data insights. When you have an ongoing relationship, especially one that is digitally supported, you gather content and

behavioral data that can be analyzed to improve AI and everyone's experience. Think of the Netflix recommendation engine.

- Build a new revenue source. Subscriptions provide a better idea of month-to-month revenue for more thoughtful investment management.
- Deepen the revenue stream of existing customers. When existing customers want to go deeper, you can provide greater access, advice, or the assurance that they won't miss out.
- Protect your customers from competition. If customers join and trust you to deliver on your forever promise, they'll be less likely to shop for alternatives, creating a barrier to disruption.

Why the Business Case Matters

It might seem like overkill to answer all of these questions before doing any kind of in-market test or product launch. Too often, organizations lack the discipline to design a test that will actually move the company forward because they aren't specific enough about where they want to go. As a result, the success criteria are vague, or the team lacks the resources to test effectively, or they move too slowly.

Companies often call me to help them with the incubation phase before they've developed the business case. I'm told that the board and CEO fully support the idea of membership, services revenue, subscription pricing, or going direct. In reality, leadership may loosely support one or more of these concepts, but the organization hasn't defined what these concepts could mean for the company, and/or what the costs and payoffs might be. Or worse, they see subscription pricing as a box to tick off, without considering the array of implications. Moving to subscription pricing without considering other

> Moving to subscription pricing without considering other necessary changes risks customer backlash, cannibalization, and corporate distraction.

necessary changes risks customer backlash, cannibalization, and corporate distraction.

Putting Your Business Case Together

To ensure a solid foundation, I encourage companies to devote a few weeks (usually at least 2 and no more than 12 weeks) to fleshing out the business case before proceeding. After all, the objective of testing is to assess the viability of the model, make necessary adjustments, and get the green light to move forward at a broader level. Without understanding the business case, how will the organization know whether the tests have been successful?

Template: Your Business Case for the Forever Transaction

When you go to your board or leadership team to make a case for investing, you need to answer the following questions. I usually put these questions into a PowerPoint presentation, like I did back when I was a consultant at Booz Allen Hamilton, and then work with the client to figure out how we're going to fill in the pages. You can do this on your own and include some or all of the following key questions:

What's the Business Rationale?
- What's the financial opportunity?
- How does it fit with our strategic vision?
- How can it help our marketing—building relationships, prospect trial, insights?

What's Our Forever Promise?
Who are we targeting, and what are our goals? What's in it for them, and for us?

What is our vision? If we refocus our business on forever, what would it look like in three years?

- Products and services?
- Competitive advantage?
- Financial impact?
- Positioning for the future?

What Do We Need in Order to Execute on the Vision?

Why wouldn't we dive into executing on the full vision immediately? What don't we understand yet? For example:

- What's the right offer?
- How do we execute?
- What additional resources, skills, and technology might we need?
- What's the upside/downside to revenue, gross margin, CLV, etc.?
- What would it cost us?
- Who will want it?

What Are the Risks of This Strategy?

- Cannibalization?
- Backlash from customers and partners?
- Competitive response?
- Team support?

What Early Steps, Research, and Tests Are Needed?

- What questions can we answer without a minimum viable product (MVP), through research?
- What is the MVP, and what questions will and won't it be able to answer? Features? Pricing? Scope? Target?
- What are the success criteria that would indicate we're onto something?
- Under what circumstances will we shut down the team? Under what circumstances will we expedite?
- What are the second, third, and fourth tests? We know they may not be right, but we should start thinking about them!

What Are the Criteria for Board Support?
- What support is the board willing to give us now?
- What results do they need to justify continued support?
- What metrics and milestones will be used to assess success?
- Are these proof points going to be enough to get their full support moving forward?

Assembling this business case through answering these questions will help in many ways. You may decide the business case isn't powerful enough to justify moving forward. That's useful. If your business doesn't have sufficient resources and needs to prioritize investment over short-term cash flow, that's OK. It's important to get clarity and not waste time doing more research, testing, and implementation than you need to move forward.

Performing this business case exercise also documents the best, most focused thinking about many topics that routinely pop up at leadership meetings. There are many "goals of the moment," which can all be considered and either incorporated or abandoned through a thoughtful business case assessment. Boards may ask companies to go direct-to-consumer, generate more services revenue, implement a subscription or membership model, or just be more "like Netflix," whatever that means. These requests, coming in one after another as unique ideas, can distract the whole organization.

Having a detailed business case can lay some ideas to rest or clarify the expected results and the real investment costs. By synthesizing the analysis and accumulating information on what's required, your organization can move forward more quickly.

> Having a detailed business case can lay some ideas to rest or clarify the expected results and the real investment costs.

It's likely that your board and leadership will love your business case mapped out as above, step-by-step. By defining initial steps and milestones, you are setting the stage for sufficient support before initiating testing and research. This is especially important if you're accountable for the success of the incubation period. Just because leaders sound enthusiastic or give you a verbal green light doesn't guarantee your success. Verify that you've secured what you'll need.

Don't assume leadership of your team's initial experiment in the Membership Economy until you can answer all of these questions. I'm serious. I wouldn't take on a consulting project without answers to the following questions (and my career isn't on the line like yours may be!):

- Is this a top priority for leadership?
- Am I confident that if I need resources or help, leadership will come through?
- Do I understand why and how this initiative aligns with our company's strategic vision?
- Has everyone agreed on the success criteria, and recognized that the first experiment isn't going to achieve the vision?
- Does leadership understand the principles of the Membership Economy and accept that we might lose money before we start accruing predictable revenue?

This step is critical. Be clear about needs, next steps, and timing before diving into the research and testing phases.

What to Do Next

- Create the template for your business case. Don't worry if you can't fill in everything at first.
- Scope the information you'll need to complete the template; you'll use the remaining chapters in this part to guide brainstorming, research, and analysis.
- Get agreement from the leadership and the board that, with this business case complete, you'll have what you need for a go/no-go decision.

4 Define Your Forever Promise

On July 8, 1889, the first issue of the *Wall Street Journal* hit the newsstands. It was born of the so-called "flimsies," or "slips": bulletins that its parent, Dow Jones, messengered to Wall Street financial houses multiple times per day.[1] Over time, the *Journal* has expanded globally to deliver in-depth articles and features in multiple languages, in both print and digital editions. It offers conferences and experiences, tools and data in addition to content. But its promise hasn't changed—everything is still built around trusted facts and viewing the world through a business and markets lens to help readers make informed decisions.

Forever is a long journey. As in a successful marriage, both parties make a commitment, a promise. Your vision serves as a North Star, guiding your team. That vision and promise needs to be valuable enough to your best customer to justify a recurring payment commitment.

If you dive into specific subscription pricing and features without establishing your vision, forever promise, and best customer, you risk launching an offering that doesn't achieve your goals or those of your customer.

If you dive into specific subscription pricing and features without establishing your vision, forever promise, and best customer, you risk launching an offering that doesn't achieve your goals or those of your customer. Or, success with your initial trial offering might lose momentum because there's no guide to the next step. It can be tempting to bundle existing products and features under a membership banner, but this muddies the value proposition for your prospective customers. Having a low-cost subscription or membership doesn't mean anyone wants it.

To determine the core direction for your forever transaction, do the following:

1. Articulate the *promise* you make to customers through the transaction.
2. Define your specific *customer*. Your forever promise isn't going to serve everyone. Distinguish between the people who will become your best customers and those who won't.
3. Outline your *vision* of the fully realized model and its value to your best customers and the company.

This chapter guides your team through these components of your North Star.

Your Forever Promise

A forever transaction happens when a customer starts behaving like a *member*, is committed to your organization, and stops looking for alternatives. The member (at least mentally) turns on autopay and stops worrying about this expense. Different businesses justify different "forevers"; it's important to logically define yours. Tie your promise to an industry standard only if you're promising the same thing as everyone else.

> **Different businesses justify different "forevers"; it's important to logically define yours.**

Sephora offers the greatest variety of makeup with in-store attendants, while Rodan + Fields offers a more limited selection of dermatology-inspired skin care products with dedicated independent consultants. If you love sampling all the latest beauty products like an insider, you might be a member of Sephora's VIB Rouge program for decades. R + F's selection is much smaller than Sephora's, but their products address specific and long-term skin concerns. Both companies have highly engaged members who trust these organizations to deliver on their promises—the hallmark of a forever transaction.

Every organization *wants* forever transactions with customers. People complain that "these days customers are fickle, and that loyalty isn't a value." This isn't true. The forever transaction demands and deserves loyalty from both parties.

You Can't Justify a "Forever Transaction" Without a "Forever Promise"

Your first task is to define the promise underlying your forever transaction. Many companies want recurring revenue but won't commit to deserving the customers' trust. There is a serious ethical component to the promise; it's not enough to simply meet legal requirements. You must feel that if the customers heard your rationale, they'd trust you even more. If you believe the customers should "read the fine print" if they want a good deal, this model isn't for you.

A forever promise is different from a brand promise. A brand promise tends to be company-centric. It says, "You can always expect us to build this kind of product, to communicate in this way, to position ourselves relative to our competition like this." A forever promise focuses on what an organization's target customer can expect. Customers don't want product-centricity or company-centricity. They want an organization that will evolve with their needs, incorporating current available resources. They want a promise that the company will solve a problem or create an opportunity forever.

Consider the promises behind Netflix and HBO, companies with clear audience commitments. Netflix's forever promise is access to the largest selection of professionally created video content, optimally delivered, with cost certainty. HBO has been uniquely competitive with Netflix. It promises access to a narrower range of critically acclaimed, original content. These are differentiated but individually successful promises—volume and ease vs. high quality—that guide the companies' strategies, product development, and messaging.

HBO's narrow but powerful content drove tremendous subscription revenue growth as the market for subscription video content exploded with players like Amazon Prime Video and Hulu (majority owned by Disney). Bloomberg.com says, "Shows like 'Game of Thrones' drove subscriptions; between its debut in 2011 and 2018, HBO's subscription revenue went from $3.8 billion to $5.6 billion, generating $2 billion in annual profits."

Forever promises can be at the mercy of leadership—customers aren't the only fickle ones. After AT&T's acquisition and the departure of CEO Richard Plepler, who guided this effort, the new leadership shared a new strategy. According to Joe Nocera's *Bloomberg* article, HBO was directed to create content in greater volumes, with less of an emphasis on quality. And Netflix has recently spent billions on high-quality original content. That's a distinct change in the forever promise of each.[2]

Your Best Customer

Your forever promise has to appeal to your best customers. A new organization may not have pinpointed a best customer. Start with a best guess of your sweet spot. Who will derive the most value from your forever promise and be most willing to pay for it on an ongoing basis? Consider demographics and psychographics, but also think about their need states. What will trigger customers to sign up, and what results will keep them engaged? For example, if you've never really been sick, even if you can afford concierge medical care, you might not want it—that's often the case with offerings that mitigate risk. You might decide to join after yet another primary care physician moves out of your provider network, leaving you to find someone new. But you might stay with concierge medicine because of the level of white glove treatment and breadth of service. These are two very different things—I call the drivers to join "triggers" and drivers to stay "hooks."

Write down and prioritize your hypotheses. You might conduct research to fine-tune or launch an initial forever transaction offering and track results. The more hypotheses you want to test, the more people you'll need to reach, and the more experiments you'll conduct. If budget is tight, begin with a focused hypothesis and adapt as you learn.

A more established business likely has some idea of its better and worse customers. The best are likely to be happiest with your offering and recognize its value. They are the customers you most desire and around whom you want to optimize your forever transaction.

Identify some of the actual individuals who are your best customers. Evaluate those with the highest customer lifetime value (CLV) and develop hypotheses about their shared traits. Although demographics and psychographics might be the most obvious, you'll find additional insights if you examine

> The best customers have the greatest customer lifetime value (CLV); they will spend more with you over time than anyone else.

their *behavior*. What channels did they come through? What messages resonated? How did they onboard? How recently, frequently, and deeply have they engaged? Compare best customers and worst customers—those you acquired who weren't ultimately profitable or who weren't satisfied with your offering. Notice people who exhaust your free trial but don't convert to paid, or who join but cancel within the first few months.

Produce either a qualitative write-up of your best customer or use regression analysis to prioritize characteristics. Share these conclusions with your frontline team—retail workers, customer support, sales—to accrue early insights. With a concrete conception of your best customer, you can discern if the customer segment is sufficiently large to justify addressing. Test and adjust as needed. Then make these best customers and their forever promise as "real" as possible to the team. If you have actual customers who fit the profile, talk about them, invite them in, or have their pictures on your wall. You're going to feel their pain, share their objectives, and design experiences for them. It's important to know them well.

Finding your forever promise and best customer are part of an iterative process. First, determine who your best customer is. What biggest group would get the most value from your products and services and would be willing to pay a fair price for that value? Then, define the deeper, underlying need this group wants you to solve, forever. (Hint: It's not to have your product.) Frame it as a "promise" and test with your best customers. Are you correct about its importance? Iterate until you start gaining traction.

Your North Star Vision

Your vision inspires and motivates the team to slog through the challenges of transformation. It's the picture you paint as the leader—the worldview after you've done the research, the initial trial, the iterations on product, and the tough negotiations and conversations with partners and colleagues.

Begin by imagining what your forever promise would look like if fully realized. For example, video game company Electronic Arts (EA) envisions a "player first" ecosystem absent all the friction limiting a player's ability to maximize game-playing enjoyment, particularly having to invest $60 or so just to try out a new game! CEO Andrew Wilson wants to "connect a billion people in play."[3] EA has made significant progress toward realizing this vision. Its player network makes it easy for players to connect for competition and learn about and evaluate new games. EA's paid subscription offerings, EA Access and Origin Access, encompass most of EA's best games accessible via PC and video game consoles, costing a fraction of owning the games outright. With this vision in hand, EA has a clear path for future development work: attracting the world's players, optimizing games for streaming, and introducing new titles continuously to maintain player engagement.

The beauty of a vision like this one is that it's clear and compelling, and just out of reach. It must remain a touchstone for the organization after the minimum viable product has been released. Achieving that early milestone is crucial but is only the first step in following your North Star. As its name suggests, the forever transaction is a journey, not a single transaction. It is critical to have a guiding principle that keeps you moving forward.

Different Approaches to a Forever Transaction Around Wine

Imagine trying to design a wine club as a forever transaction built around wine. What will your forever promise be? You could offer the widest selection at a fair, fixed price with easy shipping, like K&L, the largest wine retailer in the San Francisco Bay Area. Its inventory comprises several thousand wines acquired worldwide. You could offer access to exotic exclusives. You could offer a great sense of belonging. You wouldn't need to promise everything to everyone, though.

K&L has a flexible approach. Members pick reds or whites or German Pinots and their price point. But they don't pick the specific varieties. The forever promise might be "the easiest way to try new wines you'll like and can afford." There are regular shipments, but no ongoing relationship with a single winemaker. That promise might be "Never run out of the wines you want, whatever they may be."

Other wineries sell their best wines to members of their wine clubs, depending on loyal and discerning fans for the cash flow that justifies future investment. They sponsor special events for members only—crush parties or wine and food pairing dinners with local chefs—sometimes charging extra fees, sometimes not. These wineries promise true membership: "Join us as we make and enjoy great wines."

Still other wineries focus on the winery experience. Members picking up orders might "cut the tasting line" even on busy days. The winery might offer members tastes or snacks while orders are packed. This approach generates a sense of belonging and status while providing value. The promise might be "You'll always be an honored guest."

Even for distant customers, membership can keep people current with their favorite winery, receiving an allotment of the best wines, even those made in limited quantities. Members may receive a discount and personal recognition from the winemaker.

Many features could be incorporated into a wine membership, depending on the forever promise being made. Features around wine deliveries include:

- The number of bottles in a shipment, from one to many
- Frequency of shipments: monthly, quarterly, biannually, annually, or as needed
- Type of wine: a choice of varietals or inclusion of everything produced as options

Features around pricing include:

- A fixed shipment for a fixed price. Cost certainty can be great with an implicit promise of value at that price. Unfortunately, fixed shipments may feature the highest price point options, taking advantage of the member's trust (and credit card).
- Tiered pricing. Members might choose from a range of price points, with all purchases enjoying member discounts. Among clubs with varied price points, it's rare for members to be allowed to set a maximum spend per shipment. There's always a risk of exceeding budget.
- Premium Membership. Members pay a fee up front for the privilege of accessing deals whenever they want. This approach is similar to that of a Costco membership.
- Loyalty Program. Members earn points and benefits based on depth and frequency of purchase, similar to airline and hotel programs.

Features at the winery might include:

- Ability to collect your purchases in the winery, often with a free tasting

- Invitations to special events, included, or for additional fees
- Unlimited tastings, perhaps of premium wines and/or without advance reservations

Whatever features you choose, the members should be your most engaged customers. They've proactively chosen to prioritize your wines over other options. You need to ensure they're satisfied with their experience and feel like they're getting the best deal. Many people move to subscription pricing because they want price certainty and a cap on spending. It's surprising how many wine clubs are unable to fix a spending cap on each shipment.

One winery, famous for some of the best rosé in Napa Valley, doesn't include rosés in its memberships. Instead, it sells rosé to restaurants and retailers. Its member tastings don't include rosé, either. This winery may be using membership to unload less popular wines at no discount. In other words, it treats its members *worse* than it treats strangers. Its members are benefactors, paying a premium out of altruism, without any recognition. If members trust this winery, they might be surprised and disappointed to discover that their membership procures less value than that provided to an anonymous customer.

> Many people move to subscription pricing because they want price certainty and a cap on spending.

Here are a few dos and don'ts if you want your membership to have deep engagement and long-term relationships. I used a wine club as an example, but note that these principles apply to many kinds of recurring revenue businesses:

Don't take advantage of your most loyal customers.

Do make your members feel special.

Don't bundle in irrelevant "gifts" because you happen to have them, instead of focusing on the value that aligns with the forever promise.

Do send the occasional pleasant surprise and make your members feel like insiders.

Don't exclude the best products and services from the membership unless that's a specific selling feature. Membership is all about trust.

Do look for ways to reduce friction. Make the entire process transparent and easy.

And absolutely *do not* hide the cancel button. In any subscription model with automatic payments, the exit needs to be easy. That's ethical; why would you want to make money when you know people aren't deriving value? Even from a mercenary perspective, organizations are finding that the revenue gained by extending subscriptions via a difficult cancelation process is offset by negative impacts to the organization's reputation. If customers struggle to cancel, they're less likely to rejoin or recommend.

Remember, members should be surprised by the quality of the experience and the special value you provide, and not by being charged more than expected. Their trust should never be abused. It should be rewarded!

What to Do Next

- Step back from your products and services to consider the bigger promise you're making to your best customers. What problem are you going to solve for them, or what goal are you going to help them achieve, forever?
- Imagine what your customers' experiences might be if you fully realize your forever promise. What benefits would your customers enjoy?
- Determine who your best customers are, and more importantly, who they *aren't*.

5 Choose the Right Who for the How

At this point, you're probably thinking about who should be involved in both the exploration and possible implementation of your forever transaction. The best person to shepherd a company's launch into a membership model is not necessarily the same person who established the vision. Nor is that same person always best suited to run the fledgling business post-launch. Startups may find that existing leadership is well situated to manage multiple business phases as the organization is smaller, the infrastructure simpler, and the transition less complex. Larger, established companies have layers of operational specialists and may benefit from team reinforcements.

Organizations of all types and sizes must be aware that different leadership skills may be needed for successive stages of strategy rollout. To be successful, you and your organization should envision the process in distinct phases, and you need to assign the right team members at each phase.

The best person to shepherd a company's launch into a membership model is not necessarily the same person who established the vision.

Phase 1: Launch

In this early phase, you'll need a team to develop and win support for the business case, as well as to conduct the testing and learning before scaling the initiative. All of these tasks might be completed by the same person or team, or they might be more specialized, depending on the size and structure of your organization. When you're just developing support for the business case, you'll need strategic expertise, often coming from consulting, finance, and/or entrepreneurial backgrounds. This team can develop a clear, substantiated argument for investing in a forever transaction. Along with a range of skills to build the business case, you will need subject matter expertise around building and running "forever transaction" businesses. Adding a membership model or incorporating subscription pricing can be difficult to figure out as a neophyte. If you lack this resource internally, look on your board or consider hiring outside help.

Next comes testing the offer in a limited way before broadly committing to operationalizing the model. The testing team incorporates functional experts to execute implementation across sales, marketing, operations, and product, along with strategists. It might have the same leader as the business case phase, or a more hands-on entrepreneur to ensure that any existing business-as-usual is not impacted, *and* that the testing team can act quickly.

Phase 2: Scale

Once you have a green light to accelerate and scale the implementation into a key part of the business model or the core of the company's strategy, you'll need a change-management leader who can juggle multiple work streams, outside consultants, and robust internal communications. This "transition team" should be staffed with operationally focused, full-time members pulled from the functional departments and tasked with management of a multiyear project. They also need a passion for customers and entrepreneurial spirit.

Phase 3: Lead

Completing the marathon of operationalizing the vision to market at scale is just the beginning. You must resist the temptation to dramatically reduce the team, cut the budget for continued innovation, and/or transfer the attention of executive sponsors to other projects once this initial phase is complete. Operating at scale involves a huge learning curve about acquisition, engagement, and most importantly, churn. Take nothing for granted until you figure out your company's unique churn. For a year or two, it's imperative to nurture this sapling business, not starve it.

The following story of Hagerty's transition to a forever transaction illustrates the roles of the different leaders and the handoffs between them.

Case Study: Three Teams for Hagerty Drivers Club*

I spent several years working with Hagerty—the world's largest provider of collector car insurance—as it established a membership model for car lovers. Hagerty wanted to provide offerings beyond insurance and roadside products that added to the enjoyment of car ownership or participation in the automotive lifestyle, regardless of whether the customer needed classic car insurance or even owned a car.

Hagerty was an ideal candidate for a forever transaction for two reasons. First, many of the people who insured their classic cars through Hagerty already called themselves "members" because of strong brand affinity. Second, as a privately owned business (the company was founded by the parents of the current CEO, McKeel Hagerty, in 1984), Hagerty is committed to the community, the members, and the brand, well beyond short-term revenue.

---

* The bulk of the content for this story come from the author's work with Hagerty, and from interviews and emails with McKeel Hagerty, Nancy Flowers, Eric Okerstrom, and Eric Kurt, Spring 2019.

McKeel Hagerty, the former chairman of the International Board for the Young President's Organization, is serious about creating a family legacy. He is the ideal CEO for a forever business, understanding that building a membership model requires both investing for the long term and several types of leaders over the course of the journey.

Launch Phase: Eric Okerstrom

McKeel* tapped Eric Okerstrom to research and lead the exploration of membership. Okerstrom was familiar with McKeel's vision; leaders at Hagerty had discussed creating a membership type of organization for years. In fact, McKeel had once expressed that if he could start the company from scratch, it would offer insurance and other products and services within a membership framework. The company has a reputation for exceptional service, insurance, and related products. The leadership viewed membership as an avenue to better serve clients and expand Hagerty's reach into the car enthusiast market. This approach resembles USAA, which provides car insurance to service members. Hagerty, however, would focus on people who love cars and driving them.

Okerstrom's first task was to assemble a team and define what membership would mean at Hagerty. He says, "Someone has to take the idea and ask, 'What does this really mean for our business?' You must get clear on it; discuss and share it with the right people for feedback and ultimately pitch it to others for approval. For example, this is what the customer or potential customer would experience, what it would be like and perhaps most importantly, why they would join. I think you have to have this first." It took about 12 weeks to articulate a few different options for a Hagerty membership model, including three tiers, a range of pricing, and a financial model for testing assumptions and scenarios. Again, this phase cannot be rushed.

This phase was about vision and strategy. It required a charismatic and credible forward thinker to define the big picture and persuade the

---

* Because it's confusing to call the CEO and the company both Hagerty, McKeel Hagerty's first name is used, while everyone else is referred to by last name.

board, leadership, and organization to tackle this difficult challenge. Okerstrom was the right person for the job. "When we completed this phase," he explained, "I was confident I could tell the membership story to anyone at Hagerty and they'd get it and know why we should do this."

Okerstrom could see that he wasn't going to scale what he was scoping, nor would he run it, but he owned the vision. He garnered approval from the board for the resources to flesh out the plan and begin implementation. Because company leadership already had a membership mindset and confidence in the strategy, and because they didn't want to confuse their insurance clients, they bypassed a small test, implemented the Drivers Club broadly, and integrated it into their business processes.

Then Okerstrom's colleague, Nancy Flowers, took the wheel.

Scale Phase: Nancy Flowers

I got a call from Nancy Flowers in June of 2015. I had met her briefly during my earlier work with Okerstrom. Flowers had been tapped to spearhead the next phase: design, development, and implementation of a new membership offering. This entailed everything from product features and branding, to technology requirements and business readiness.

As with any major initiative, change management was essential. Hagerty wasn't just launching a product; it was adopting a new way of operating and thinking.

As McKeel said, "We are transforming from an organization primarily focused on insurance to an automotive lifestyle brand that puts members at the center of everything we do. This is about a mindset shift, and it requires every person at Hagerty to think differently."

A major part of Flowers's role was to engage every level of the organization "There is just never enough. I really don't think you can over-communicate or over-involve when facing transformational change." She recommended establishing a framework and rhythm that included all methods and channels of communication, emphasizing employee involvement.

The initiative was strategic and spanned a few years, requiring consistency and repetition. Leadership had to be reminded that long-term retention and revenue were more important than initial acquisition results, that the product offering must align with the pricing model, and that customer "need states" and behaviors needed to be tracked. Flowers's team conducted multiple organization-wide education initiatives. Many organizations under-communicate because team leaders wrongly assume the organization tires of hearing about the initiative. With consistent, persistent communication, Hagerty team members understood that participation was part of their job, not a favor granted.

Technology presented another major challenge to implementing the new business model, typical of this major transformation. One of Flowers's hardest hurdles was to guide Hagerty in becoming a technology company.

Early on, the team selected a narrowly-focused "membership technology" solution to support the launch of a membership product. Midway through the project, they realized that Hagerty needed an enterprise technology platform capable of supporting *all* aspects of a rapidly evolving business, including but not limited to membership, into the future. Pivoting to a sophisticated enterprise software solution broadened the focus, introduced more complexity, and temporarily delayed the launch of the Drivers Club, but it was the right decision.

In retrospect, Flowers says she would have asked for "more of everything—more technical support, more time, more people. . . . I think we underestimated the enormous task of changing our business model and launching a new product on top of our day jobs of keeping a very healthy, thriving business running."

Lead Phase: Eric Kurt

During implementation, Eric Kurt was designated to take over as the ongoing overseer of Drivers Club, which made for a smooth transition. A product management and sales leader, Kurt had the skills and relationships to run a business for Hagerty and had managed Profit and Loss (P&L) Statements before. Kurt joined the team as Nancy got close to launch.

This was a particularly ambitious launch to both existing and new customers. Integrating the experience with the current interface was complicated, and the team knew that existing customers might encounter a choppy experience. Many companies face this tough decision—you want existing customers to have early access to the "cool new membership," but backward integration is much harder than a fresh canvas. As previously mentioned, younger companies and startups have an advantage integrating a membership model into their strategy from the beginning.

Already known for treating customers like members, Hagerty leadership was committed to treating their existing customers at least as well as new ones. Leadership worried that existing customers would feel shortchanged if their transition experience was inferior to or later than that of new members. Transitioning the existing pool would be a huge undertaking. Even aligning renewals for both insurance and the Drivers Club was hard. It was important to the Hagerty team that existing customers got the best pricing, which meant that they couldn't offer introductory discounts as incentives for new members. Additionally, they had to figure out how to integrate the new benefits into the existing member experience before they could launch with new members, to ensure that there was no inadvertent penalty to existing customers who wanted to join.

Despite the obstacles, the implementation phase resulted in the successful launch of Hagerty Drivers Club. The team received additional resources to continue developing the program with regular improvements. Unlike insurance, the Drivers Club is a fluidly changing offering that involves continuous tinkering, different than Hagerty's historical quarterly and annual rhythms.

> You want existing customers to have early access to the "cool new membership," but backward integration is much harder than a fresh canvas.

Hagerty's story holds lessons for any business attempting this transition. Specifically, the company installed people with the right skills for each phase of the project, choosing leaders who communicated effectively with their teams and the broader organization. In smaller organizations, the same person may have responsibility across multiple phases. Regardless, it's important to recognize the changing needs at each phase, and to explicitly evolve goals as the business grows.

Communication Is Key at All Phases

Team members must have connections permeating every part of the organization, unearthing potential inconsistencies and dependencies and keeping everyone aligned.

Some parts of the organization will invest many hours to build the model. Key performance indicators (KPIs) and incentive plans may demand adjustment to support these novel roles and the implications of the new model:

- Marketing defines the member journey, what happens during the acquisition, onboarding, engagement, and retention phases, and how to talk about and price the new offering. This entails market research, analysis, and many spreadsheets.
- Product teams innovate a minimum viable product (MVP) that can take the team to the next phase. They should also establish a loose road map so the team knows where to go next, like a GPS showing the three turns beyond the next turn leading to your destination.
- Sales teams determine how the change in product will alter the selling process.
- Administrative teams in HR, legal, and accounting will investigate legal and reporting issues; finance validates assumptions and predictions made by the team.
- Operations modifies organizational processes and coordinates with the technology team to ascertain what can be automated and what can't.

Consider having a team member, whether employee or outsider, who has experienced this process before to anticipate where issues might arise, offer reassurance that challenges are normal, and ring alarm bells when the undesirable happens. HR should honestly evaluate gaps between the current culture and the desired future state. If you don't have a person on your team who can do this, consider an outside advisor or allocate time

TABLE 5.1 Teams for Transformation

	Launch—Business Case	Launch—Incubate (optional)	Scale	Lead
Leadership	Strategic	Entrepreneurial	Change management project manager	P&L owner
Goal	Business case	Proof of concept	Systems, culture, consistency	Business health
Skills	Market research Competitive analysis Product design Financial modeling	Prototyping Market testing	Project management Operations Tech requirements and implementation Communication	Corporate innovation
Challenges	Making something from nothing Getting a green light (support, understanding, and engagement of board and leadership team)	Cutting corners Sequencing tests and features How minimum is still viable? Keeping engagement and support of leadership	Building support and engagement across organization Changing culture and dealing with pushback Implementing new tech without impacting existing customers Risk of cannibalization	Underinvesting Backsliding Focusing too much on acquisition or retention

for the internal team lead to reach out to people who have had similar experiences who might serve as mentors.

At Hagerty, Flowers's task force (scale phase) included the CIO, the head of content, and the head of brand, as well as about a dozen midlevel managers from finance, marketing, and operations. The head of HR periodically joined to ensure the organization grasped the cultural implications of the membership. It was Hagerty's first offering available to customers who didn't own a classic vehicle. Okerstrom (launch phase) was involved at the outset to ensure a seamless transition, but later quickly moved on to unrelated projects.

It's crucial to incorporate membership as the new normal across the organization. This is true transformation, far beyond "change management" as usual. It requires engagement from every functional area. Flowers sums up Hagerty's success: "We knew from the beginning this was about changing the way we think more than anything else. That success comes from putting the members at the center of our decisions and actions. While getting the product right was key, it had to be about creating solutions to meet members' needs and adding value to their lives. So yes, at the end of the day it *is* cultural."

What to Do Next

- Identify your team lead for the phase you're in.
- Determine what skills you need that you do not have in-house for your current and future stages.
- Build a team of advisors (from outside your organization if necessary) who have experience with customer-centric, recurring revenue dependent models.
- Network externally with other companies that have successfully transitioned to a recurring revenue model.
- Allocate budgets and hours generously enough to ensure success.

6 Develop Your First Experiments

In 2014, Electronic Arts (EA) was among the first movers in gaming to bring a subscription service to life with EA Access, a subscription offering available via Microsoft's Xbox One console. While subscription business models seemed attractive to the company, the path to this future was unclear, given EA's historical strength with individual games. Electronic Arts was one of the world's blockbuster developers of video games. Players bought a game or two annually at about $60 each, usually the latest release of their favorite franchises. EA games ran the gamut from sports to shooters to strategy games, from FIFA to The Sims. These blockbuster successes were part of the problem though. Players waited for the new releases. Business was transactional, seasonal, and heavily dependent on promotions. CEO Andrew Wilson wanted to focus on how to more effectively help players find and play new games in the most player-friendly, ongoing manner.

Migrating to subscriptions required instilling a "player-first" mindset to benefit both players and the business. If EA continues to create great entertainment, subscribers will stay and play. When players stay, EA gains greater insight into how they play, nurturing delivery of better games. The players find new games to explore as they await updates to their favorites. As a thriving business, EA had a lot at stake in changing business models. The company needed to be careful and invest in thoughtful testing and learning.

Michael Blank, an experienced EA executive, was tapped to lead the subscription project, but with the mandate to proceed cautiously. Blank's team needed answers to pressing questions: Could EA offer subscriptions without cannibalizing existing revenues? How would EA avoid alienating valuable, powerful partners: retailers like Target and GameStop, and console manufacturers like Sony and Microsoft?[1]

At the same time, the team couldn't suddenly change the way the company designed games, with major releases every year or two. Before this strategy would be revisited, Blank's team had to demonstrate to the leadership team, through step-by-step testing, that the company could successfully leap to a subscription pricing model with a member-oriented approach.

There's always fear around cannibalization—that current "best customers" will transition to a less expensive subscription and lighter customers won't upgrade to subscription.

Initially, the initiative was "off to the side" away from EA's core business. The first subscription was for an Xbox One subscription to a catalog of older (about six months post-launch) games. This was followed by numerous experiments and research. Eventually the team tested an offering including new releases and availability for PC games.

EA's use of subscription to achieve its forever promise of being fully player-first is not yet completely realized, but it's well on its way. Says Blank, "Five years after our first subscription launched in 2014, we continue to learn as we go. What we know today is that players play more and stay engaged when we give them frictionless access to great content in one place. We know we are on the right path and are focused on keeping players as our first priority as we build for the future." EA is now the leader with subscription services on more platforms than any other gaming company (three platforms:

PlayStation, Xbox One, and PC). But the journey began with a small test.

Start Small and Learn

It took Netflix years to expand nationwide in the United States, have original programming, or become available via digital streaming. LinkedIn was once just a place to easily post your résumé. Most companies, even those with the biggest promise of a forever transaction, start small. They have to.

A modest launch may be due to limited resources—not enough staff, money, or time. Sometimes entrepreneurs are stymied by ambiguity or lack of clear direction. The organization may resist disrupting a specific target audience before they're confident. There's always fear around cannibalization—that current "best customers" will transition to a less expensive subscription and lighter customers won't upgrade to subscription.

Resistance from partners, investors, and peers can also pose significant challenges. If you're moving from hardware sales to selling services—particularly subscription services—you must balance the product team's needs with the investment requirements of the streaming business. If you're bypassing retailers and wholesalers to go direct to cus-

> It's easier to adjust your strategy than to move forward with no strategy at all.

tomers, you may get too much pushback to move forward successfully. Overcoming these challenges requires mapping out a step-by-step path for your own business launch or transformation.

Break down your longer-term vision for membership into small parts so you can begin making progress. Specify the steps that will get you there and whether they require research or an actual in-market product test. Each step must naturally transition into the next. It's easier to adjust your strategy than to move forward with no strategy at all.

Get entrepreneurial: begin testing ideas with prospective customers, through both market research and actual testing of product prototypes. One useful model for product testing is the well-developed and documented concept of minimum viable product (MVP). Dan Olsen, the author of *The Lean Product Playbook*, describes the MVP as "The smallest set of functionality that delivers your product's value proposition that has been validated with customers." He cautions teams to "avoid taking on too much scope too early with your product" but also "not to use this as an excuse to rationalize a shoddy user experience or a buggy product."[2]

The "Getting Started with Forever" Brainstorm

You're more likely to suffer from too *many* ideas, not too few. There are so many subscription and membership options available. Many organizations will want to include a laundry list of features that they've seen in other people's offerings—such as discounts, content access, exclusive experiences, concierge-like services, "surprise and delight" features, and even a cool membership card. They want immediately to offer multiple tiers and maybe even some kind of points-based currency.

But while all of these features might work, it's important not to let the tail wag the dog. Features serve different purposes for the customer and might lead to a different outcome for your organization. Someday, you may be able to invest in providing all of them. For now, that's too ambitious—it would take too long and cost too much. Start by working toward a modest test, while keeping in mind a long-term vision of what you'd do if you had unlimited time, power, and resources. Make sure your test is clearly linked to the long-term vision.

Get clear on what phase you're in—are you brainstorming for the first time the full range of possible features and benefits, or prioritizing? Or are you executing on decisions that have already been made, to determine the most cost-effective and powerful way to test your hypotheses?

Many of my clients get stuck between brainstorming and prioritizing. Yet they want to jump ahead to testing and validating without first exploring the possibilities. Brainstorming is an important part of the process. Team members should take into account organizational considerations, customer considerations, and alignment with the forever promise as they evaluate the potential hypotheses to test.

You can do a first pass on all of these questions in one day with a small team. Make sure the brainstorming questions include not only the ideas in the room, but also ideas that other stakeholders and influencers have contributed. If the CEO always talks about how the company needs stickier relationships with customers, or to attract a more youthful audience, incorporate those objectives into the brainstorm. You don't have to chase down the CEO's pet hypotheses, but you do need to consider them. You need a good answer for why you prioritized as you did.[3]

> Acknowledge all the unspoken risks and fears explicitly, so your colleagues and investors know you're aware of them and taking them into consideration as you move like crazy down your narrow early path.

Acknowledge all the unspoken risks and fears explicitly, so your colleagues and investors know you're aware of them and taking them into consideration as you move like crazy down your narrow early path. The summarized brainstorm, coupled with winnowed-down recommendations, can translate into a huge leap forward in your process.

Making Sure Your Test Delivers

Next, a team member should synthesize all of the data in a test, including a few options along with their specific risks and mitigations. Based on your brainstorm, you can start putting together your test. Dan Olsen has mapped out a range of options in the two-by-two matrix he uses for MVP evaluations (Figure 6.1).

	Qualitative Tests	Quantitative Tests
Marketing Tests	Marketing materials	Landing page/smoke test Explainer video Ad campaign Marketing A/B tests Crowdfunding
Product Tests	Wireframes Mockups Interactive prototype Live product	Fake door/404 page Product analysis and A/B tests

FIGURE 6.1 Tests Categorized by Type[4]

Many experts limit tests to the types in the lower left corner—Qualitative/Product tests—but I agree with Olsen's assessment that other types of activities can be equally valuable early stage experiments. The important objective in this phase is to make sure that the experiment you design answers the right questions and points the direction moving forward. Most organizations neglect this step.

For example, if your goal is deeper engagement among existing customers, don't waste time on features designed to attract new customers. If the target members are moms with school-aged kids, you won't need discounts at late-night clubs. And if you're selling wearable devices, like Apple, and you're targeting an audience that's 50 percent women and seeking health tracking, it might make sense to track menstrual cycles—something Apple's research teams notably forgot.

> The important objective in this phase is to make sure that the experiment you design answers the right questions and points the direction moving forward.

Identify the Risks and Roadblocks for Learning and Leverage

There are many compelling reasons why companies don't go all-in from the outset and why early testing is so important. I divide these roadblocks and risks into two categories: *learning* and *leverage*. Learning objectives bolster internal confidence. Knowledge breeds confidence; without it, organizations won't invest heavily in a new initiative. The team leader might say, "Even if money were no object, I'd want to do a smaller test or roll out the vision piece by piece. I have a lot to learn before I invest."

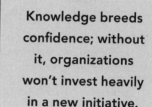

Knowledge breeds confidence; without it, organizations won't invest heavily in a new initiative.

Learning objectives can answer these questions:

- Are my best subscribers who I think they are?
- Is my platform scalable?
- How do people engage in our community?
- How long do people stay subscribed? What drives churn?
- What does it cost to service subscribers?
- What is the most important benefit that will trigger sign-ups?

Learning objectives come from *within* the team.

In contrast, leverage objectives are achievements or milestones necessary for the team to get the green light. They mitigate the risk of deeper investments. Achieving these goals gives your team the proof points, beachheads, or authority to move forward in ways that other stakeholders might attempt to obstruct. Leverage objectives originate *outside* the team. Table 6.1 lists possible leverage objectives sorted by the stakeholders that might impose or require them.

TABLE 6.1 Possible Leverage Objectives

Leverage Objective	Stakeholder Who Needs It
Critical mass of customers	Distribution partners who might be upset by a direct-to-consumer move
Demonstration that existing revenue cannibalization is revenue	Colleagues with P&L responsibilities
Validating processes to justify operational and IT investments	Operational and IT teams
Demonstrating long-term, predictable revenue impact to justify investment	Board, CEO, CFO
Sufficient subscribers to support a vibrant community	Existing subscribers

Determine which objectives you must achieve to prevent push-back from other stakeholders. Your team must address them to build a trial for long-term success. Identify these critical objectives so you can resolve them.

Prioritize Learning and Leverage Goals, and Achieve Them in the Right Order

You'll notice that some of your listed objectives need to be met before you can advance at all. To move the needle on engagement, you need to demonstrate that people will consume more of your products and services with the new model. Perhaps the first step is proving that people would find your offer compelling. Your priorities will depend on whether you need to justify the bigger investment, or whether you plan to work stealthily to build consensus before launching in a public way.

Whatever your priorities, remember that you don't need to build your offer out fully in order to learn. Sometimes you just need research and not a full-blown test. For example, to prove the perceived value of the offer, you don't have to build *all* the features—you only need to design the marketing offer. One of my clients who was exploring a subscription music offer created an email campaign for existing (transactional) customers with the subscription features and pricing. Anyone who clicked all the way through in the first few hours of the test learned that the product wasn't real yet and received a $10 gift card, as well as thanks for their response.

Another client wanted to test a concierge feature, a call center of experts to provide advice and connections. Given the small test volume, the task force took those calls directly so they wouldn't need to hire concierges before understanding expected call volume and the nature of the requests.

With your forever vision, a proposed starting point, and a clear set of objectives, you're ready to deploy and learn from your first steps toward forever.

> With your forever vision, a proposed starting point, and a clear set of objectives, you're ready to deploy and learn from your first steps toward forever.

What to Do Next

- Gather your most creative, strategic, visionary, and passionate team members for a "getting started with forever" brainstorm.
- Make a list of all of the possible features you could offer your best customer(s).
- Determine what would be free, and what would be paid.
- Determine what research you can do immediately.
- Begin scoping the first, smallest offering you can test, and what specifically you will test.
- Outline the next several steps that will add to your learning and your ability to build leverage with other stakeholders to support your plan.

7 Test, Learn, Adjust

Once you've developed the parameters and objectives of your test, it's time to implement it in a way that helps you acquire the learning and leverage required to go further. It's not enough to just conduct that first test—it's likely the first of many iterations, tested rapidly. You need to build momentum to propel you on the journey toward your longer-term vision. It's time to get entrepreneurial.

Communicate your Compelling Vision for Membership

Even with a green light from leadership, you must educate key people organization-wide to understand the vision and their roles in achieving it. Team members, partners, and eventual customers must be persuaded that this complex path, significant investment, and effort is justified by the outcome. Success is most likely when everyone embraces the strategy.

Articulate the compelling vision. Add images to illustrate it and, if you have them, work with your data scientists, market research, finance, and operations teams to buttress the vision with numbers. The plan won't be exactly right—it's unlikely even if your business is wildly successful. But it's critical to make nebulous ideas more visceral and verify that the logic holds when all the pieces are assembled. When your colleagues can see and understand the vision of where you're headed, they are more likely to get on board.

Even with a green light from leadership, you must educate key people organization-wide to understand the vision and their roles in achieving it.

Realistic expectations and effective communication are essential to excite the team about the mission and motivate them for the possibly arduous journey ahead. Brett Brewer, General Manager, Microsoft Office Growth, has actually developed his own courses and onboarding materials to educate his colleagues about the unique challenges and processes needed for success in the Office 365 subscription business.[1] According to Brewer, a big part of why his team created a "Subscription 101" type of curriculum was a realization that functional departments like marketing, finance, and product development don't operate the same way for software-as-a-service as they do for manufacturing. In other words, if you have subscription pricing, you need to think differently about all departments. In fact, Brewer points out that universities are now asking him and other business practitioners to guest lecture on these concepts. It seems many academic institutions have yet to catch up with modern business models because the world of subscriptions is evolving and growing so rapidly.

Case Study: FabFitFun

FabFitFun (FFF) launched in 2010 as a newsletter. Today, it's a $200 million lifestyle brand complete with major financial backing and global strategy. It offers members a quarterly subscription box, access to a vibrant user community, and original content delivered by newsletter, magazine, blog, and its newest live TV channel, FFFTV.

FabFitFun launched with a consistent mission and built out the robust membership business it is today. The mission—FFF's forever promise—is described on its magazine site: "FFF aims to motivate, inspire and excite readers with a slew of great, healthy resources for every kind of woman—from the new college student to the new mom."

Begin by describing what you'd do if you could invest in your ideal subscription model immediately, without any constraints. For FabFit-Fun, that vision includes inspiring *everyone* from college student to new mom. What would it look like if it truly provided great healthy resources for *every* kind of women, including older moms (like myself) or women whose education ended with high school?

FFF might have envisioned these features at the outset:

- Content (text, image, video, audio)
- Product
- Education (classes, trainings)
- Live events
- Global community of women inspiring women with user-generated content
- Coaching by professionals and/or by peers—everything from personalized styling to fitness to relationship advice

Obviously, FFF didn't implement this full vision initially, and you don't have to either. Few companies know enough and have the resources and confidence to do everything at once. Remember, Amazon started as a bookseller, and Netflix only carried other people's movies and TV shows.

Start Small and Keep Adding—
Don't Do It All at Once*

When FabFitFun launched in 2010, founder and chief editor Katie Kitchens had many questions. Her list of learning and leverage objectives was long.

She needed to see if her promise appealed to her target audience, to learn what it would cost to attract them, and what it would take to engage and retain them. She needed to prove that the audience would spend money with her brand, although it wasn't yet clear whether that would be content or products. If she wanted to sell physical products, she had to figure out which products, how to procure them, and whether they'd be exclusively hers or a curated collection.

Despite FFF's bold "forever promise," its first offering was modest—a newsletter. Even today, with a global footprint, television, branded products, and nearly a million members on its Facebook page,[2] the company has infinite room to continue traveling toward full realization of its lofty goal. Step by step, it layers in greater value, stronger infrastructure, and new functionality to actualize the vision first defined in 2010. It continues to add benefits for its members, augmenting "how" it delivers on its forever promise.

The Electronic Arts (EA) story from Chapter 6 provides another example of this progression. After conducting successful small tests to validate its minimal viable product (MVP), EA initiated a second phase of experimentation, which entailed testing hypotheses for future scenarios to answer pressing, *long-term* questions:

1. Would subscription pricing cannibalize their business? Would the subscribers be those who were already buying multiple games at $60 every year, or would the offer attract casual players and entice them to spend more time and money?

---

* Dr. Nathan Furr and Paul Ahlstrom provide great insight about how to do the right things in the right order when scaling in their book *Nail It Then Scale It*, https://www.nailthenscale.com/.

2. How would console manufacturers and retailers react to a strategic pivot?
3. How would game players react if they got access to new releases ("frontline games") in the subscription?
4. Would different regions of the world respond differently to a subscription offer?[3]

Phase two took more than a year because the team needed to observe player behavior over time to evaluate the impact of the subscriptions on game play patterns. The phase two offer included most of the company's games, new releases as well as the catalog titles, at a low price of $14.99 per month or $99.99 per year.

Again, the test was limited to players using PCs, a small percent of overall customers. The primary goal was to increase engagement among, and deepen the relationship with, existing EA customers. This effort was not oriented to bring in new customers, although the team believed that new players would try the service because of its overwhelming value. The company believed that the more deeply subscribers engaged, the more value they'd get from their game time, naturally resulting in happier subscribers and greater revenue.

Learn from Early Failures

Many organizations abandon their forever journey early on because of a perceived or real failure.

Most of these failures come from a poorly designed test. If you don't define the goals of the test (revenue vs. signups vs. engagement, for example), how will you determine if the test "worked" or not?

I've seen companies "test" subscription by making their existing catalog of content available at a monthly price. When people binge the first month and then cancel (what I call a "smash and grab"), the company views the test as a failure. *Is* it a failure? Not if the question was "How will people consume our content if they have unlimited access and pay by the month?"

> Try to pinpoint whether your failure is due to a communication problem, a product problem, or an execution problem.

Some companies perceive general success when what they've proven is narrow. For example, you may prove that people will use something you give away. That's engagement. It doesn't prove willingness to pay. Those are two different things!

Even if your experiment is well defined, failure can illuminate remedial actions to get you on a right path, one you might not have expected. Try to pinpoint whether your failure is due to a communication problem, a product problem, or an execution problem.

TABLE 7.1 Three Common Causes of Early Failures

	Communication Problem	Product Problem	Execution Problem
Definition	Prospect/customer doesn't understand what you're offering or how to maximize its value	Prospect/customer doesn't feel you've delivered on your promise (most expensive to fix)	Customer experience is clunky and contains feature gaps
Examples	Campaign targets the wrong people OR Value not explained in a clear and compelling way OR Customers sign up but then don't know what to do next	A wedding dress of the month club OR A meal kit targeting busy young families that is too spicy to appeal to most children and/or too complicated to prepare quickly	A streaming content company has unreliable streaming technology OR A makeup company offering "everything you need to look great" doesn't include lipstick

- A *communication* problem occurs when the customer doesn't understand what you're offering or how to maximize its value. Or, the initial offer triggers people to sign up, but attracts people who might not find value in the subscription. You might not be reaching the right people or explaining the value in a clear and compelling way.

- A *product* problem is when people understand your promise, but don't feel you've delivered on it. For example, you promise a monthly box of great outfits, but most of the outfits don't fit or look good on the subscribers. Or your app is supposed to let marketers manage their own website, but it requires coding—a skill most marketers lack. Or perhaps you made a pricing error that needs to be adjusted. Fixing product is more expensive than improving communication.

- *Execution* problems result when the product experience is clunky and has feature gaps. I worked with a streaming content company with unreliable streaming technology. People were losing connection in the middle of the soccer championship. Great promise (live streaming of games). Great

> ∞
>
> **Fixing product is more expensive than improving communication.**

product (an app on your phone that streams content). But the thing just didn't work! This happens more often than you might think. In an era of ready-fire-aim and MVP, sometimes the offer is *less* than what is minimally necessary. In these cases, the organization might fix the execution problem and then retest. That's why it's important to bound the size of any trial so you can test in additional markets if the first one fails.

Incubate and Learn

This incubation and test period differs for every business. Some organizations use this early phase to define their ideal forever promise, develop best practices for operations, and optimize pricing. Other companies take different approaches. Some launch in a single market. Some start with pricing much higher than they expect to use at scale, so they don't risk cannibalizing an existing business. Some launch with a single feature, planning to add later—like Amazon did with books. Who remembers that Amazon launched its "all products for all people" e-commerce platform with a single product category?

Nike Adventure Club—Nike Experiments with Direct-to-Consumer New Business Models

When I told Dave Cobban, general manager and cofounder of Nike Adventure Club, that I wanted to include their story in this book because I wanted to ensure there were examples of subscription box models, he quickly corrected me. "We're not a subscription box company—we're giving parents the ability to access brand-new kids' shoes in easy and convenient ways. We are more akin to a leasing than transaction model—and we're recovering those shoes at end of life and either donating to foster kid programs or recycling through Nike Grind."[4]

This "circular business" concept was initially tested in 2015 with runners who swap out old shoes for new ones after about 300 miles of use. Runners loved the idea, but parents among them reported: "This would be great for me, but even better for my kids." Most parents hate the hassle of shopping for kids' shoes every couple of months.

The kids-focused Nike Adventure Club (initially called EasyKicks) was launched in August 2016 through Nike's Advanced Innovation Team.

Nike's Intrapreneurial System Uses a Launch-Leverage-Lead Model

After researching various incubator models, Nike developed a model similar to Launch/Scale/Lead:

> **Launch.** With early "angel" funding, Cobban validated the business problem, solution, and business model.

Scale. Nike got first right of refusal to "buy" the startup, investing financial and other resources as well as contributing brand muscle to scale to profitability.

Lead. Once the business achieved goals established by one of Nike's business leaders, it was integrated into the organization.

Launch: Proving the Adventure Club Model

The original EasyKicks model was simple. For $20 a month, parents could swap their kids' sneakers as frequently as desired. Used sneakers were returned for donation or recycling. Nike kids' shoes average $60, so with a three-month cycle, revenue would remain the same, with a hoped-for deepening relationship and increased share of shoe purchases.

The EasyKicks team soon realized they had two candidates for their "best customer":

- Convenience moms, who swap shoes every 60 to 90 days
- Proud moms, who swap shoes frequently *and* act like superusers: tweeting, Instagramming, and making lots of referrals

Convenience moms were the anticipated audience. Proud moms were a surprise, with a totally different forever promise, revolving around fashion.

The startup team made major choices. They changed the pricing structure, which is difficult to do. In 2018, they conducted a multivariate test, experimenting in market with four pricing options at once. (Cobban tells me that Rent the Runway and ClassPass do similar testing.) But they encountered some unexpected challenges from which they were quickly able to learn. The internet is a transparent marketplace; people quickly discover if there are multiple concurrent offers. EasyKicks received many customer support contacts from people saying, "Hold on, you offered my friend a better deal." But the team learned a huge amount in a short time.

The pricing model that "won" the multivariate test had three tiers, but it still included the unlimited offer:

- Order new shoes every 90 days for $20 a month (base offer)
- Order new shoes every 60 days for $25 a month
- Unlimited swaps for $30 a month

Acquiring customers with this new pricing taught the team two key things:

1. People like choices of plans; it anchors them in the deal they want. Experimentation demonstrated that three choices are optimal.
2. Unlimited plans are cost prohibitive. As MoviePass has learned, it's impossible to predict how often people will use the service, so costs keep rising over time.

In April 2019, the EasyKicks team pivoted again toward more limited "fixed offer" plans and incorporated the ability to pause and upgrade. This facilitates customer flexibility while ensuring fixed service cost for Nike.

They tested this new formation while still branded EasyKicks to verify there wasn't false data associated with the inclusion of the better-known, already trusted Nike Swoosh.

Scale: Use the Power of Nike to Reach All Kids

In July 2019, EasyKicks rebranded as Nike Adventure Club. At this point, the team's scale-up strategy evolved to include a deeper invest-ment in relationships with children as well as moms. The informal motto became "recruit the mum, retain the kid."

Shoe shipments started including adventure challenges, an adventure journal, and adventure cards with instructions for playing "old school" games like four square or wall ball. Additionally, the company began campaigns promoting the creation of user generated content (UGC), such as images of outdoor games unique to specific locales suitable for posting on the Nike site.

**Lead: Continue to Experiment with Membership to
Sustain a Forever Transaction**

When Adventure Club reaches a predetermined target revenue and profitability, it will integrate into Nike's North America business with global expansion likely thereafter.

Contemplating how the model might expand across the organization is fascinating. Cobban notes that the membership model still makes great sense for the original intended audience—runners. He believes a significant proportion of Nike's future business could eventually be driven by the Membership Economy. For Nike to have ongoing connections to its customers without dependence on third-party retailers would be a huge shift in culture and strategy. Cobban thinks membership could unlock that potential.

The Risks of *Not* Maintaining Momentum

Nike has been disciplined about a phased but aggressive approach to experimentation. Maintaining momentum can be challenging, though. Many organizations lack the focus and energy to quickly build on successes and adjust for early failure. Moving too slowly can result in missing the opportunity entirely. Here are some snapshots of companies that didn't leap in with both feet:

- *The hardware manufacturer* that had a small success in services revenue but didn't apply additional resources. Instead it focused its energy on promotions to encourage existing customers, in a saturated market, to upgrade the hardware, which had a bigger short-term top-line revenue impact. Since hardware upgrades are optional, transactional (one time), and not terribly profitable, the company missed the bigger opportunity to fan the flames of its nascent recurring revenue services business.
- *The enterprise software company* that started building, in 2008, a "light, SaaS-structured" offering for smaller, nimbler prospects.

Its product leverages the cloud and is optimized for subscription, but it was never rebuilt from the ground up. Consequently, it lacks capacity to track behavioral data and allow subscribers to configure their implementation. Meanwhile, the sales team continues to sell the on-premise solution—which 80 percent of them prefer to do because they earn higher commissions on those sales. The organization regressed from ahead of the curve to behind it and now risks missing the wave altogether.

- *The newspaper* that offers a subscription but is "hedging its bets" through continued dependence on a traditional advertising model. The two models directly conflict; the old ad model requires a large audience that pays only with their eyeballs. The subscribers want relevant, useful content. To maximize views, a paper might use a picture of Kim Kardashian, but content worth paying for is more likely to be a deep analysis of the bond market.

- *The consumer packaged goods company* offering a replenishment-based subscription model, delivered in ugly, hard-to-open boxes, with complex pricing, no relevant educational materials, lousy support, and terrible returns. This company missed the opportunity to make the experience better than other channels, by personalizing it or creating a deeper connection, or at least making it fun and delightful to open.

Subscription pricing in a vacuum won't get you to a forever transaction. In Part Two, we'll talk about building the organizational infrastructure to move fast, accelerating and turbocharging your growth.

Keep the Momentum

As your team analyzes the trial balloons, it should articulate what constitutes success and think beyond first steps. If things look good, what's next? You may take progressively bigger steps before the entire transformation is complete or you publicly announce the strategic change.

Don't revel too long in the success of your small experiment before pushing for the next giant step. Know before you launch your test that if it's successful you will quickly be able to scale. There's nothing more frustrating than a "successful" test that won't scale, or one that lacks momentum.

Most organizations assume the rest of the world isn't going to change as fast as their own organization will. Remember: everyone's trying to ride that same current. If you're pushing hard to build this new model without identifying why it's special for the people you serve, you're not going to stand out. Nearly every company I've spoken to in

> **Know before you launch your test that if it's successful you will quickly be able to scale.**

recent years is experimenting with a forever transaction and a recurring revenue relationship with its best customers. That alone is difficult, but you must also determine how that forever transaction can be expressed broadly through a more fully developed offer, more systemic delivery, or a larger audience.

Before launching your initial experiment, you articulated a compelling vision of where your organization can be "someday." This forever vision probably includes some combination of community network, subscription pricing, direct-to-consumer connection, and sophisticated content. You'll probably require a new technology platform to support deeper customer engagement, more sophisticated pricing strategies, and better analytics. All of this happens before you realize the benefits of additional revenue sources.

If you didn't flesh out this vision earlier, do so now. You need to have a perspective of the future and how to anticipate transformation; you must envision a strategy beyond "keeping up." How will your forever transaction provide a beachhead for your next phase of organizational growth? Just doing "the basics" takes significant investment.

Leadership and colleagues across the organization may want to slow your progress. They may put roadblocks in your way. You may be the only person in the organization scanning the horizon and envisioning how this transformation can get you there. Clarify the strategic journey and make it compelling for your colleagues. Help them understand the payoff, but also the high cost of moving slowly.

What to Do Next

- Develop a specific set of believable hypotheses that you are trying to prove or disprove before launching broadly, both to feel confident about your plan and to build support from other constituents (partners, colleagues, customers).
- Determine which hypotheses you can answer from the early tests and which you won't.
- For hypotheses that you cannot answer with your trial, brainstorm ways to research and approximate your answers.
- Make sure you're testing the most important questions first. Design future tests when you have had a chance to absorb the learning.
- Create a plan for your first few steps so you can retain focus and momentum as you conduct your first tests. You don't want to lose focus as you wait for the results to come in.

PART TWO Scale

Many organizations that experiment with membership models, subscription pricing, or recurring revenues don't successfully scale up from the foundation of their hard-won experimental results. This part is designed to help you accelerate the momentum of your experimentation phase to grow your business. Perhaps your early efforts here have been ignored or underinvested. Or maybe joining the Membership Economy is a high priority for your board and CEO, but you're not sure how to move beyond the startup phase without negatively affecting the rest of your business.

Now is the time to speed up by investing in infrastructure, marketing, global expansion, or new offerings. Whether you're a start-up entrepreneur, a publicly traded company, or a nonprofit, this part provides the strategies and tactics you need to accelerate your growth, without sacrificing customer relationships or "betting the farm."

There's a lot of heavy lifting in scaling your business. My goal in Part Two is to help you leverage the experiences of hundreds of other companies. You'll need these best practices as you scale forever across your organization.

Chapter 8: Manage Emotions, Transform Culture, and Build a Shared Vision

Chapter 9: Do Acquisitions Make Sense for Your Company?

Chapter 10: Six Common Setbacks and How to Avoid Them

Chapter 11: Choose the Technology to Scale

Chapter 12: Create and Fine-Tune Your Pricing Strategy

Chapter 13: Essential Metrics for Long-Term Relationships

8 Manage Emotions, Transform Culture, and Build a Shared Vision

I love my Peloton bike, and not just because the company has been part of the Membership Economy since it launched. Peloton bikes come with an attached tablet computer that streams live spin classes, and riders can compete with one another on a leader board, simulating an in-person class, without having to leave home. All of the classes are also available in the Peloton catalog, so you can ride anytime. It is currently my favorite way to exercise.

I find the instructors supremely motivating. They offer inspiring exhortations:

"Don't stop when you're tired. Stop when you're done."

"Pain is temporary. Regret is forever."

"No one said it would be easy. They said it would be worth it."

These expressions hold true when it comes to building a forever transaction. In other words, it's hard. Pain should be expected as part of the package and welcomed as a sign you're really committed. The results—recurring revenue, loyal customers, a disruption-proof model—are worth it. Think of building a forever transaction as a journey. You have a general idea of where you're going, a North Star. That's your forever promise. You have an idea of what to pack—some subscription pricing, some customer success, a product that's continually improving and evolving, communication and community to support your members on *their* journey. You've heard stories, read books, and prepared well. And you've been out to the frontier, testing your ideas through your initial experiments. But now it's time to bring the rest of the party along.

So far, you've successfully created the map and packed the bug spray for the mosquito-ridden swamp. You recognize that you might not make it to your ultimate goal unbitten. This chapter offers some guidance to make the journey easier, by making sure that everyone traveling with you shares your resolve and knows what you know. Now it's time to build the culture.

Managing Emotional Roadblocks

You should expect emotional roadblocks as you scale. Some employees across the organization will resist for emotional reasons, even when they understand the *rational* reasons for the new strategy. It's your job to empathize first, then respond, and ideally, inspire.

Your colleagues might have feelings like these:

- I don't believe this is the right path for our company, so I'll just ignore it and hope it goes away.
- I don't want to learn new required skills because I'm scared I'll fail.
- I enjoyed faxing documents/working the printing press/unhitching the horses and am resentful that the earth is shifting beneath my feet.

People are afraid of what change might mean for them personally— who they might have to work for or with, and how their personal power might diminish in light of changing politics. Emotional challenges are difficult to recognize and remedy in part because they might sound foolish, irrational, or selfish. People don't speak them aloud or may lack the words to articulate how they feel. It's easier to change what people do than how they feel. Consequently, your team members might do what you ask but without enthusiasm and while dragging their feet.

Examples of these personal, emotional concerns that might slow you down include:

- Product teams may not be inspired by the new customer-centric direction because it means the products won't impress their peers or win industry and association awards.

It's easier to change what people do than how they feel.

- Sales stars might resist a farming model when they've made a name for themselves as big game hunters. They may fear compensation clawbacks* if the client doesn't embrace the product or chooses to cancel early.
- Operations and IT are no longer gatekeepers for all new technologies, due to the influx of software-as-a-service (SaaS) offerings that don't require IT implementation, customization, and support.
- Experienced marketers may resent the move toward data-centric campaigns focused on engagement and retention and away from "creative" tasks, acquisition activities, or the hunt for new logos. Different skills are required, and the work is less glamorous.
- And finance may worry about the transition to subscription cannibalizing today's revenue, driving investor outcry, as well as confusion about new and changing subscription rules and revenue recognition.

One B2B software company's CEO told me his Asia Pacific sales director had earnestly explained to him *in 2019* that companies in his

---

* A "clawback" is a contractual term that provides that money paid to an employee be returned in situations where the objectives weren't achieved.

region "were not ready for subscription." Yet Asia is selling SaaS like crazy! Salesforce alone did $10 billion in revenue in Asia Pacific in 2018.

> There's a huge amount of emotional risk involved in this change, particularly among longtime and senior employees.

You'd think by now, with so many subscription businesses, that employees would be excited to make this transition. However, there's a huge amount of emotional risk involved in this change, particularly among longtime and senior employees. They may disguise their fear as misunderstanding, logical objections, or unavoidable delays. Usually, it's just fear.

Where to Dig for Hidden Emotional Landmines

Most companies dramatically underestimate the time, effort, and resources it will take to transform their business from a transactional, product-centric, often offline business to a model focused on business outcomes and customer needs.

For a mature public company, this transition might take as long as five to seven years to be fully realized, according to J. B. Wood, CEO at the Technology Services Industry Association (TSIA).[1] A smaller, more nimble organization might see major results within the year. The road map, investment, staffing, rate of change, etc., is vastly different between the two. And during this transition phase, it is common for the financial investment to outweigh the revenue generated, resulting in what Wood has termed a "fish model" (Figure 8.1), in which costs rise and then fall while revenue falls and then rises, leading to a graph that resembles a fish. It is much easier, less noticeable, and less expensive to prune a sapling than a huge oak; the same is true of newer and smaller organizations.

The software industry is the most sophisticated at understanding the importance of aligning the long-term customer goals with the long-term organizational goals around a "forever promise" based on outcomes, not features or products. Wood estimates that 95 percent of his

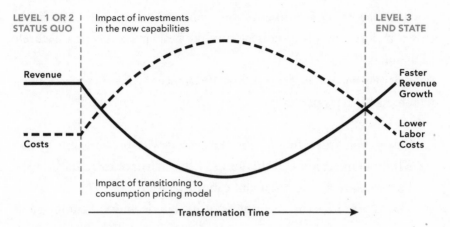

FIGURE 8.1 "Fish Model" of Cost and Revenue Changes
Source: Technology-as-a-Service Playbook 2016 (TSIA)

member companies have successfully transformed in one of the following ways:

- From transactional (perpetual licenses) to cloud served to SaaS
- From selling to a technical buyer to selling to the business buyer
- From selling features to selling outcomes

Companies like Oracle, Microsoft, and Adobe (the poster child for successful transformation from an ownership model to an access-based subscription model) have learned to "burn the boats" in moving to a SaaS model, lest employees try to return to the safe ground of their former business model. (You can read more about their journey in Chapter 20 of *The Membership Economy*.)

When digging for emotional landmines, start at the top. Leadership sets the tone with the board. Do the board members understand that transformation is going to take awhile? Are they comfortable with declining revenue in the short term? Do they have the stomach for losing some of their non-core customers?

Even in organizations where everyone knows their members or customers are demanding a new business model, and that their current model is becoming a dinosaur, your colleagues may drag their heels. This transformation is usually a "run like hell" process, not a leisurely excursion.

You may have an undercurrent of resistance if you find the following symptoms in your business:

- Salespeople still swing for the cheap seats with big one-time deals.
- Midlevel managers call this strategy the "flavor of the month."
- People express concerns about cannibalization.
- Teams prioritize the needs of longtime but declining customers, unreflective of the future, over the demands of prospective new customers.

If your organization is scrambling quarterly with promotions and deals to hit targets, there are people whose incentives aren't aligned, or who are afraid or unwilling to transform. The sooner you find them and fix the emotional leakage, the better.

The Reluctant Hardware Company

I recently spoke with a mid-level manager at a large organization that had built a successful business selling high-end connected healthcare devices. Its board wanted the organization to incorporate services to smooth out revenue and increase the organization's valuation. This perspective—membership as a means to drive short-term revenue and valuation—is a red flag.

The executive sponsor developed a membership strategy with a subscription model, based on a compelling forever promise: living your best life by optimizing your key health metrics. They had a blueprint for a minimum viable product through which a services subscription could be launched and a road map of additional features to test and learn from over time. It was a logical, doable strategy. The product team, marketing team, technology team, and finance team supported the plan. The plan was easily justified on the basis of long-term revenue and expected value to shareholders. But the transformation was likely to take a few years—investment was required and cultural change too.

As it turned out, the CEO was working on a key performance indicator (KPI) that defined success as implementing "a membership strategy" within the year. So the organization jettisoned the strategy and did a small, points-based loyalty program instead, offering discounts on accessories and not much else. It doesn't matter how good the strategy is if the KPIs don't align with the CEO's incentive structure.

A Cultural Shift to a Member Mindset

Committing to a forever promise may require a cultural shift in your organization. Instead of focusing on Profit & Loss (P&L) statements by product, you'll be centering your success metrics around your customers. It's not enough to get the sale—you need to optimize for engagement. You might need to educate your team members, both across your organization (even leaders) and newcomers to your specific team, on "Membership 101."

Even some senior leaders may not understand this point of view—business schools haven't caught up yet. Says Brett Brewer, General Manager, Microsoft Office Growth, "All of the accounting and GAAP principles were taught around making widgets, not subscriptions. All those things that we live and breathe aren't being taught with the same rigor."[2]

It doesn't matter if the customer doesn't characterize herself as a member, although this might be an aim; the *organization* must think of customers as members—people they know, with whom there's an ongoing expectation of a continuing relationship. If you've ever had an anonymous driver honk at you and then realized that the person knew you, you understand that we feel differently about offending a stranger than someone in our community. Employees treat customers differently when there's a personal relationship. This means that organizations need to put customers at the center of everything they do.

> Most subscription businesses that fail do so because they don't understand that for subscription pricing to work, they need to establish a trusted, forever transaction with the subscriber.

Some organizations are *product-centric*, optimizing around the products they create—a car company or a software company, for example. In a subscription model, subscribers have greater flexibility to cancel, so the product needs to continually evolve to remain relevant to customers. Most companies *claim* they put the customer's needs first, but this is rarely true. Some companies are *revenue-centric*. They're drawn to the promise of recurring subscription revenues, but disregard that the pricing change necessitates a new business model and not just new pricing.

A revenue-centric business strategizes to maximize financial results in the short term. In a transactional, product-centric business, focusing on meeting quarterly numbers can be effective. For example, adding fees to the product increases revenues. However, ongoing subscribers expect pricing to remain consistent and are angry (and might cancel) if fees are added, especially without commensurate functionality increases. Many companies sacrifice long-term subscriber relationships for short-term revenue and as a result their business fails.

In February of 2019, Kraft Heinz Co. disclosed a $15 billion write-down in intangible assets, including once-beloved brands Kraft and Oscar Mayer.* Many following the company believed that this loss in value resulted from the company's longstanding focus on cost-cutting. While this approach managed profitability in light of increasing costs for commodities and transportation in the short term, ultimately Kraft Heinz neglected its commitment to provide high-quality food at a fair price. Kraft is not a Membership Economy organization with a

---

* A "write-down" is a reduction in the estimate of the value of an asset.

customer-centric orientation; it's an example of what can happen when an organization is too revenue-centric.

Most subscription businesses that fail do so because they don't understand that for subscription pricing to work, they need to establish a trusted, forever transaction with the subscriber. The customer needs to be treated like a member, like someone who will be interacting with the company for the long term. The company needs to join the Membership Economy.

How do you know if your company has the right mindset? One way is to do what customer experience expert and author Jeanne Bliss calls the "Make Mom Proud" test in her book *Would You Do That to Your Mother?*[3] She wants company executives to think about how their mom would feel as a customer. Talk about a "long-term relationship" you don't want to damage!

Here's another clue: companies with a member mindset have a balance between acquisition metrics and retention metrics. Acquisition metrics tell you if your promise is appealing enough. Retention metrics (churn rate, customer lifetime value or CLV) indicate whether you're delivering on that promise and if that promise truly justifies forever. Many companies prioritize acquisition over retention. That's a misplaced mindset.

Many companies prioritize acquisition over retention. That's a misplaced mindset.

What a Customer-Centric Business Looks Like

I'm always skeptical when an organization claims to be "customer-centric," a very popular term right now. Organizations oversimplify what it means, believing that all they need to build a forever transaction is new tactics, like subscription pricing or a membership product, and some new marketing language. They may not envision the systemic and cultural challenges they face. If you know what to look for, you can assess a company's customer-centricity in 15 minutes (or less). Table 8.1 offers a few clues, but I encourage you to take the time to answer the questionnaire.

How Customer-Centric Is Your Organization?

YES	NO	
☐	☐	We care more about the relationship than the transaction.
☐	☐	Our top two metrics are customer lifetime value (CLV) and customer happiness or Net Promoter Score.
☐	☐	We always speak as if the customer were in the room with us.
☐	☐	Our staff has some leeway to take care of the customer using their own judgment, going beyond standard procedures.
☐	☐	Every employee knows at least a few of our best customers by name.
☐	☐	Our organization understands and works around the customer journey.
☐	☐	Our organization has many ways of collecting and analyzing customer data—well beyond demographics and psychographics to include behaviors, feedback, preference.
☐	☐	Our customers enjoy a personalized experience—they feel a sense of being recognized and appreciated.
☐	☐	All organizational processes are aligned around the customer.
☐	☐	Our organization focuses on the marriage (post transaction) more than on the dating (marketing).
☐	☐	Everyone shares an understanding of what customer-centric means.

Now grade yourself: count one point for each Yes. Did you count 11 Yeses? Wow! Fewer than 5? Watch out!

TABLE 8.1 Product-Centric vs. Customer-Centric Companies

	Product Centric	Customer Centric
Metrics	Average transaction size, quarterly revenue	Recurring revenue, customer lifetime value, NPS
Hero Shots, Décor	Product images	Customer images
Product Development	Major releases, hit driven	Continuous evolution, engagement driven
Leadership	Looking to next role	Committed to legacy (i.e., family-run business)
Research	Focused on transaction	Focused on customer journey

Building a Shared Vision

The best defense is a good offense. Inspire people with your vision. Aligning customer and corporate goals around a shared mission, and explicitly tying your strategy to it, can be very motivating, particularly with a younger workforce.

In June of 2015, Satya Nadella sent a memo to all Microsoft employees with their new mission: To "empower every person and every organization on the planet to achieve more."[4] This vision is exciting in its breadth and ambition. For people who'd spent years toiling away at feature enhancements to Microsoft Office, or as account managers for fickle Fortune 50 Microsoft customers, this was a game changer, signaling a new way of doing business.

In nearly every meeting about strategy, Microsoft employees tie their initiatives and tactics back to this mission, checking alignment. It raises the level of conversation from "what I want vs. what you want" to "what's going to help the most people achieve more?"

It didn't happen overnight. In fact, this transformation inspired an entire book for Nadella and years of work across the entire business.[5] Brett Brewer, General Manager, Microsoft Office Growth, had to create a Subscription 101 program to educate his colleagues.[6] But Nadella's support from the top has been critical.

Strategy Is a Commodity, Execution Is an Art[7]

Culture change is probably the hardest and most underestimated challenge of moving an organization from a transactional to a membership mindset.

Ideally, you will dedicate resources to define the essential changes in culture, in functional roles, and in processes, and then educate the entire organization and specific groups on the changes that may affect them. Some of the resources should come from HR, but you may also want someone who is strong in internal communications. Some of your messages will need to be communicated multiple times, through different channels and in a range of settings: all-hands meetings, one-on-ones, department trainings, corporate email, and the employee handbook.

To make all of this happen, you'll also need support and a steady drumbeat from leadership to ensure that this transformation, while difficult, will pay off in the long term. Without clear, consistent support from the C-suite, you're likely to fail.

What to Do Next

- Make an honest assessment of your organization's current culture, whether you're just getting started or have a strong, well-documented, and intentional culture.
- If your organization has a mission, vision, and values statement, put it on the wall, get a few colleagues in the room, and discuss whether a stranger visiting your organization would recognize these statements as true.
- Identify any potential problems in your current organizational structure, budgeting process, or compensation plan design that may hold you back.
- Who is being asked to change the most? Who is losing (or gaining) budget and head count?
- With your team, brainstorm about potential undercurrents that might prevent you from reaching your goals and map out strategies to manage them.

9 Do Acquisitions Make Sense for Your Company?

Evolving your entire business to a Membership Economy model can be challenging, and it can be slow. In most cases, though you'll need to build momentum as you scale. It's a huge undertaking to add skills, create a new culture, change your business model, and build a different, highly sophisticated technology platform, especially if you're transforming while still moving forward in your existing transactional business.

You may be tempted to jump-start scaling through acquisition, buying an organization that's already figured out these challenges. Small companies are more nimble than larger ones. As Peter Drucker said, "Large organizations cannot be versatile. A large organization is effective through its mass rather than through its agility. Fleas can jump many times their own height, but not an elephant."[1] Nordstrom was among the first public companies to acquire a subscription business when it bought Trunk Club in 2014. Unilever bought Dollar Shave Club in 2016. Edgewell Personal Care snapped up Harry's Razors in 2019. Under Satya Nadella, Microsoft has acquired several Membership Economy companies, including LinkedIn and GitHub, to realize his vision of Microsoft as a customer-centric company. In his book, *Hit Refresh:*

The Quest to Rediscover Microsoft's Soul and Imagine a Better Future for Everyone, Nadella wrote "We needed to build deeper empathy for our customers and their unarticulated and unmet needs."[2]

Partnerships also abound, comparable to "dating" instead of the marriages of corporate acquisitions. In October of 2018, toothbrush subscription company Quip and cosmetics subscription box Birchbox announced partnerships with retailers: Quip with Target and Birchbox with Walgreens. Meal kit subscription companies Home Chef, Plated, and Purple Carrot have all joined up with supermarket chains. (Purple Carrot's pilot with Whole Foods didn't work out, but it received a cash infusion from Fresh Del Monte Produce, and CEO Andy Levitt seems open to future deals with strategic acquirers.)

Mergers and acquisitions present unique challenges. When a public company acquires a private one, the young, fast-growing company is saddled with public company processes and controls, many required by Sarbanes Oxley.* It's like putting a 500-pound saddle on a racehorse. Then, CEOs do one of two things with an acquisition: ignore it or suck the life out of it; neither company benefits from the marriage.

> **Acquisitions are often driven by ego, not strategic fit.**

Acquisitions are often driven by ego, not strategic fit. Many executives eagerly close deals to capture the thrill and press attention of "look at the giant deal I made happen." Many organizations operate exactly the same way post-acquisition as they did before.

Without proactive integration, the acquiring organization accrues no benefits. Existing teams don't learn customer-centricity or how to use subscription pricing. Corporate infrastructure doesn't benefit from technologies and processes that the acquired company scales skillfully. Leadership doesn't grow.

---

* A U.S. act made into law in 2002 requiring a range of financial and auditing regulations for public companies.

Other organizations, eager to replicate the "secret sauce" of the acquired company, dissect the business, diffuse its team across the acquiring company, and subject the small team to parent company processes and bureaucracy. Many entrepreneurs welcome an acquisition as opening access to the acquiring team's resources—marketing channels, expertise, and budgets. Instead, they find the reality of the merger isn't anywhere near as good as imagined.

Even for organizations with healthy post-merger processes, integration takes more time, effort, and communication than leaders anticipate. Senior leadership sets the tone and must ensure that employees of both organizations feel engaged, supported, and like they have a future. Decisions need to be communicated clearly and repeatedly. Processes need to be streamlined. It's never easy, but it's particularly challenging when one company has a Membership Economy mindset and the other supports anonymous transactions without close customer relationships.

There are many reasons not to acquire, but companies do it every day. The pros can outweigh the cons in many ways.

Reasons to Buy or Build

Buying a company means you will immediately add elements you lacked internally. Revenue may be immediately accretive, providing economies of scale and/or eliminating competition.

Benefits of Buying
Through the acquisition, you likely gain one or more of the following:

- **Billing expertise:** Subscription model experience
- **Metrics expertise:** Customer lifetime value (CLV) dashboard
- **Product management:** A true tech team, experienced in digital products
- **Customer access:** A direct channel to a new segment

- **Customer insight:** Data around the target audience
- **Staff:** People with experience building long-term relationships and recurring revenue
- **Culture:** A membership mindset (in contrast to a transactional or product mindset)

Challenges of Buying

Offsetting those benefits are some significant challenges:

- Integration complexity
- Unproductive competition between groups
- Challenges retaining and engaging the acquired talent
- May still need to scale
- No strategic fit (if the purchase happened for ego reasons)

Both options have their advantages and can work. But there are trade-offs (Table 9.1).

TABLE 9.1 Trade-Offs in Acquisition

	Buy	Build
Leadership Support	Two competing leaders	Unified leadership
Team Lead	Not clear if acquiring company leader or new coleader takes on integration responsibility	Leader knows company well
Ongoing, Formal Relationship with Customer	Competency	Need to build from scratch
Target Customers	Depends	Depends
Customer Journey	Competency	Need to develop competency
Technology Footprint	Competency	Need to build from scratch
Culture	Competency	Need to evolve and deal with pushback

Why Build

If you build a completely new business model inside a large and successful organization, you may find that you can scale existing resources, customer relationships, infrastructure, and so on. In most cases these existing assets are either "not quite a fit" for the needs of the new business or, if they are, there's a (sometimes but not always justified) fear that the nascent business will leech strength from the business and weaken the parent company.

Getting attention and support from the organization can be a challenge. Other important objectives divert focus and resources. Turf battles emerge when resources are reallocated.*

Even with full board support, scaling a new business and integrating it with legacy systems and processes, while doing no harm to the existing business, is a slog. Scaling and merging an acquired business with an existing successful organization to create a single model is like a massive renovation and addition on a landmarked house. Integrating old and new, dealing with old wiring, vintage lighting, and no-longer-available hardwood floors is much harder than building a house from scratch.

Under Armour Goes Digital

Under Armour, primarily known for shirts and shoes, has its roots in technological advances in athletic wear. Its first product was a T-shirt made from the same fabric as compression shorts, a solution that emerged from founder Kevin Plank's frustration with cotton T-shirts that bunched up and gathered sweat under his football uniform when he was a student at University of Maryland.

From those sweaty beginnings, Plank built a business that expanded from making a better T-shirt to its current mission: "Under Armour makes you better." Since the company's founding in 1996, much of the focus has been on the development of performance gear, specifically on

---

* See Chapter 10 for more on the cultural challenges.

technically innovative apparel and shoes that help athletes perform at their best. But if you treat the mission as a forever promise to customers, you'll quickly see that there are many other ways to help people achieve their fitness goals. The digital world opens many possibilities.

Over the past several years, Under Armour has expanded its offerings, blurring the lines between physical and digital products. It now offers its fourth generation of connected footwear. Runners wearing certain Under Armour shoes can access "gait coaching" through the MapMyRun app, which assesses stride length, cadence of strides per minute, and optimal gaits depending on age, weight sex, height, and pace. Apps like MapMyRun provide a point of entry for long-term conversations with athletes. This approach creates opportunities for customer relationships beyond selling shirts and shoes through third-party retailers.

This business goes beyond simply increasing engagement; it generates real revenue. In 2018, Under Armour's Connected Fitness Division, responsible for web and mobile apps and paid memberships, posted revenues of $120 million, with an operating profit of $4 million,[3] an18.1 percent improvement over 2017. This digital business needs to succeed on its own, as the company reports the Connected Fitness Division separately. Connected Fitness revenue is a small part of Under Armour's 2018 sales of $5.2 billion, but it's a key bet for the future of the company.

Customer-centricity is core to the company's strategy. Chief Digital Officer Paul Fipps commented, "At Under Armour, we believe you need to approach consumers like a hotel concierge who deeply knows his or her guests. A concierge knows all of your preferences and the context. You have an incredible experience because it is highly personalized and memorable. At Under Armour, this experience means creating products that are relevant to our customers on both a personal and community level."[4]

Under Armour has made strategic acquisitions to fulfill this vision of the customer relationship, buying rather than building this key element of its strategy. Between 2013 and 2015, it acquired several digital fitness brands including MapMyFitness, MyFitnessPal, and Endomondo. This spending spree of more than $700 million connected Under Armour with millions of fitness- and wellness-oriented individuals, and a channel to build awareness and engagement and to learn about customer needs.[5]

So far, Under Armour has allowed the acquired businesses to retain their brands to varying degrees, with subtle influence from the parent brand. This is deliberate, says Michael La Guardia, SVP Digital Product. "Acquiring existing brands and aligning them with your existing brand is a delicate balancing act. Under Armour's goal in acquiring MyFitnessPal, MapMyFitness, and Endomondo was to bring together the largest fitness community in the world and reach them with Under Armour's mission to 'make you better.' We've been making gradual and subtle changes to the brand positioning of the apps to introduce the Under Armour brand to the community. Tests have shown us that if we move too fast, we risk alienating the existing audience, but if we're too subtle, Under Armour never breaks the surface of attention."

In the early years after the acquisitions, Under Armour was pretty hands-off. But under La Guardia, the company reevaluated the strategic synergies that would be realized through better alignment between Under Armour and its digital business. The founders of MyFitnessPal, MapMyFitness, and Endomondo have moved on, but the apps and their digital experiences are now being more actively integrated into the overall business of Under Armour.

As the company evolves into what they've called "a digital health and fitness community," there've been some challenges. As a company, Under Armour is structured around founder Kevin Plank's reminder: "Don't forget to sell shirts and shoes." Selling stuff is very different from building engagement and usage digital apps.

Integration posed many challenges. The companies had different structures, business models, compensation plans, and missions. In some cases, their target markets were different. There was overlap but not full alignment across customer bases. For example, weight loss is often a key part of the journey to best performance. Many of MyFitnessPal's members prioritize weight loss and management over optimal performance.

The rhythms are different. The cadence of a manufacturing company is seasonal, while software businesses might release new products and features monthly if not daily, a much faster drumbeat. The hiring pools are different, with gaps in compensation. One generates revenue and profits today; the other is part of the strategy of the future. Both businesses have a strong culture of innovation, but they innovate differently. Additionally, the kinds of people who thrive in startups sometimes don't in large, matrixed organizations.

Ultimately, acquisition may seem like a faster way to accelerate digital, direct-to-customer relationships and to build recurring revenue and deeper engagement. However, a huge amount of work is needed to synergistically integrate two organizations with different businesses and cultures. La Guardia suggests that before you jump to acquire the skills and product features you need, reflect on your mission and objectives. Consider the costs of both buy and build in the context of the current competitive environment. Either can work, but neither will be without challenges. Be prepared.

Transformation from an apparel manufacturer to digital lifestyle brand has taken a while. The first acquisition occurred six years ago, and vision work happened earlier. There's still much to do to complete the process. Under Armour's relentless focus on its forever promise, and willingness to change its methods, provides a unique advantage in building forever relationships with the people it serves.

Acquisitions Require Patience, but They Can Pay Dividends

Ironically, the most successful mergers are often the ones that take years to show a return on investment and require patience and humility as well as strategic foresight. Under Armour's La Guardia says, "If you're going to buy, you should ask, 'Am I doing this for ego, or am I willing to subordinate my ego in order to make this successful?' If the former, give it a pass. It will fail."[6]

Acquisition of a membership economy company can be a highly effective springboard to a more direct, personalized, and ongoing relationship with customers, as in the case of Under Armour. But absent the internal transformation, the acquisition won't be successful.

Remember, the acquisition isn't the goal, it's the starting point. Neither executives nor investors should underestimate the work required to reap the benefits of an acquisition. The easier route is an illusion; acquisition can be just as challenging as transforming the organization from within.

Acquisitions can be useful for a testing ground and cross-fertilization to install membership culture and building competency without risking the core business. Hopefully, these exploratory steps will help you determine whether and how to invest in acquisition as a means of scaling your vision as quickly and powerfully as possible.

What to Do Next

With your team, make an honest assessment of your organization's appetite for and experience with acquisitions:

- If you've acquired another organization in the past, how successful was the acquisition?
- Does your organization have a track record of incubating disruptive ideas that are dramatically different from those at the core of your current business?
- Can you identify startups built around long-term commitments to customers that might be acquisition targets?

10 Six Common Setbacks and How to Avoid Them

Any business that has been around for two centuries knows something about adapting to changing marketing conditions. Bonnier AB is a privately held Swedish media company founded in the nineteenth century that is now using a subscription model to tackle the challenges of the twenty-first century media landscape.[1] The company created the C More Entertainment Group, a streaming service that leverages the strength of its TV4 ad-supported television powerhouse. Facing local competition as well as international threats like Netflix and Amazon's Prime Video, the organization focused on a relatively narrow catalog of uniquely Scandinavian content, including soccer, regional movies and series, and hyperlocal and beloved news and children's programming. By 2017, C More Entertainment had hundreds of thousands of paying subscribers; it also had a significant base who'd canceled their subscriptions. The company wanted to double the number of subscribers who were paying for both TV4's traditional services and C More. They brought me in to help them strengthen engagement and retention.

When we took a closer look, we found several issues. Prior to 2017, the company had subpar streaming technology—many subscribers canceled for operational reasons. Since then, it had invested in industry-leading streaming quality, but that message hadn't reached all of the lapsed subscribers. A second issue was the fact that it solicited new subscribers by marketing a blockbuster movie title or a playoff match. This tactic attracted people who would "smash and grab"—sign up, watch the movie, and then cancel before paying. Many of the people who loved the company's offerings most, older fans of local content, weren't proficient in using the streaming service and needed help to make it a habit. Finally, C More was competing for resources with the traditional ad business of the parent company rather than building a unified strategy for long-term service of its best customers. None of these issues was a huge problem on its own, but together they exerted a significant downward pressure on revenue.

You'll face many challenges when scaling up your forever transaction. These setbacks might seem unique to your organization, but they are somewhat predictable. Ultimately C More scaled successfully, but first it had to slow customer acquisition and focus on customer lifetime value, improve its streaming technology, and tighten trials. In 2018, C More and TV4 were acquired by the telco Telia for 10 billion SEK (about $1 billion USD), which was a good exit for all. As of 2020, C More is one of the most popular streaming services in Sweden. Although the company had a rough start and initially underestimated what was needed to succeed, it pulled it off in the end.

The goal of this chapter is to help you anticipate some of the challenges that other organizations have experienced so you can proactively avoid or address them as you evolve to fulfill your full vision.

Setback 1: Organizational and Skills Gaps

Sometimes organizations attempt to support both the old *and* new way of doing things even as they scale the new way, waiting too long to fully transition. A key roadblock can be lack of readiness in a particular department. Sometimes the organization lacks people with the

TABLE 10.1 Scaling Challenges in a Subscription Model

Department	Scaling Challenges
Product	• Lack of resources or skills to rebuild the product for a subscription model • Trying to adapt the old product to meet the demands of the new "forever model" product when a complete rebuild would be the more sensible (and cheaper) option • Committing essential resources to old product requests by long-term customers • Cosmetic changes to product without rethinking how the product functions in a subscription model
Sales	• Lack of relationships with the people in their accounts who understand the new model • Lack of relationships with accounts that are a better fit for a Membership Economy model • Inability (or unwillingness) to explain the benefits of the new model • Incentives that aren't aligned with new pricing model or that don't support transformation • Challenges transitioning existing customers to new model
Operations and IT	• Lack of knowledge about which technologies will be most useful for the forever model • Failure to capture the user requirements of the new model, which often results in poor technology choices • Desire to self-build without first considering if "buy" rather than "build" is the better option (IT departments, especially ones run by a charismatic CTO, are often keen to start coding themselves rather than looking at buying ready built software—ironically usually sold using a software-as-a-service (SaaS) model!)
Marketing	• Too much focus on acquisition metrics, the historically "sexy" part of marketing, without accounting for engagement and retention, which has historically been the marketing backwater • Lack of understanding of the full customer life cycle • Failure of insight into the customer life cycle because data isn't shared between teams
Finance	• Lack of preparation for the initial revenue dip with the shift to recurring revenues • Underestimating the strong cash flow and/or initial investment required to initiate a "forever model" • Pricing based on many one-off requests

necessary skills and processes to make it work. As you move from the testing phase to a fuller transformation, you need to be ready, with the right skills for the tasks at hand.

Here are some examples, by department, of bumps that slow the transformation *after* the board commits to subscription revenue as a top priority of the company.

There are enough subscription businesses to assemble a playbook mapping out what each department needs to do and know to make the transformation. But companies still proceed as if they're the first to navigate these waters. Significant analytical horsepower has to be applied to reinvent everything, from the metrics, to progress-tracking, to processes, to team roles and functional expertise.

Setback 2: Cannibalization Concerns

Launching a subscription or membership business adjacent to a successful business in operation can be a double-edged sword. You may benefit from having access to an established, well-known brand, strong marketing channels, and sophisticated analytics and research teams, but there's a lot at risk if the transformation doesn't work.

For example, what if you sell clothing for $60 per item, but now offer a subscription for $60 a month with Netflix-like access to five items at a time? If you only activate subscribers who're already your best customers, you might lower their customer lifetime value without attracting new customers or more deeply engaging your less active customers. Even companies that *know* the future depends on transitioning to a direct-to-customer recurring revenue model worry about this transition. They fear leaving money on the table by killing the cash cow prematurely with an abrupt move to a model that consumers prefer.

Newspapers exemplify this dilemma. Most newspapers recognize that people love the convenience, searchability, and shareability of digital editions. Online media is also a less expensive way to create and distribute content. However, many of these media companies have large sunk investments in print infrastructure. Although print demand is declining, those readers who still want the physical paper are willing to pay more than digital consumers pay. The desire to maximize total revenue often prevents media companies from committing to new models. The same is true of advertising revenues.

If you're an entrepreneur whose company was acquired by a larger company, you'll probably have colleagues who worry about cannibalization. Many of my clients are bootstrapped or venture-backed startups disrupting traditional industries by focusing on building a forever transaction instead of an anonymous, short-term-oriented strategy. On acquisition, these entrepreneurs are excited to finally have the resources they've lacked.

But upon arrival at the new organization, they discover that resources are not available to them and the rest of the organization sees their business as a distraction, or even a threat.

There's some truth in these concerns. Assess the risk of cannibalization and, if possible, design early product offerings to minimize it. You want to be sure that your best customers won't be the only ones to convert to subscription—which would actually result in a lower lifetime value of best customers without increasing spend among lighter customers. One way to mitigate risk of cannibalization is to perform small tests so you know how major an issue cannibalization is likely to be. For example, some organizations limit a trial to a small regional market, so they limit their exposure. Others conduct a survey, asking both heavy and light customers if they'd transition to subscription. Another method is to price the subscription on the high side to lower the cost of any cannibalization. You may not get as much lift, but you also don't risk as much revenue. You can test and learn about usage patterns, effective messaging, and other elements that will contribute to the business's long-term success.

Setback 3: Dealing with a Middleman

Another challenge you may face, whether or not you are operating inside a larger company, is dealing with intermediaries. If your business includes a mobile app, you probably depend on the Apple App Store and Google Play Store for discovery and distribution. As a result you may not know much about who has downloaded the app. Many content providers have most of their business through cable and satellite companies or depend on movie theaters and radio play for distribution. Many product companies sell through retailers, resellers, or dealers; these entities have a more direct, personal, and ongoing relationship with customers.

Tactics like subscription pricing or membership programs can help these companies establish direct relationships with their customers. But it's risky to move all at once. For example, if all of your business goes through a single third party, adding a direct channel may be viewed with suspicion and anger by that third-party channel. Your distribution partners may view your direct channel as a competitive move. Even businesses that have established successful direct channels still sell through retailers. Customers might not be ready to move to direct. You need to be where the customer is—it's OK to nudge them toward change, but you can't force them (unless you have a monopoly).

In these cases, be clear about what you need to learn before committing to a direct relationship. Understand what kind of leverage you'd need to wield with channel partners to be allowed to continue with your direct relationship. If your business is global, you might have some markets with partners and others where you can start fresh and go direct. Build your understanding and your leverage in these markets before giving up the middleman.

Setback 4: Technology Setbacks

I've devoted Chapter 11 to the process of transforming your tech stack, so this is just a reminder about unexpected technology hurdles. It's difficult to figure out your requirements; once you actually start evaluating vendors and implementing the software, you might discover dependencies that expand the scope of the project and the number of stakeholders. Remember, your mantra should be to keep it simple and get to market with the minimum footprint. Otherwise, you might attempt such a major project that you never actually get to launch.

Setback 5: Unexpected Leadership Priorities

What if your company hits a bump in the road that is totally unrelated to the forever transaction? Someone sues you, or your key product guy is poached, or things take off in Latin America and it's all-hands-on-deck to manage demand. You need to be flexible and able to pivot, slow down, or speed up, your process.

There are two schools of thought about how the project lead should respond. One approach is the "one firm" approach, in which the project lead views the situation as if he owned the whole company and pinpoints the best thing to do. The other approach is the "advocate" approach, in which the project lead fights with full force to ensure her project wins the maximum resources. The latter approach resembles a litigator in a lawsuit, zealously representing his client's interests. The board decides but needs to hear the strongest case from each party.

Setback 6: Disappointing Results

What if you implement your experiments and expand your programs, and they don't work? Failure is bound to happen along the way. You might price your offering too high and get a lower response than expected. Cannibalization may be higher than you'd predicted. Maybe the technology itself doesn't work as promised and you have to deal with an angry customer base.

Things like this *will* happen. It's important to calibrate expectations up front, sharing plans for handling setbacks. If you have clear guardrails for terminating your efforts, then if you don't hit the guardrails, you keep going. It's important to try multiple different tests before conceding defeat. Track whether your offer is compelling enough to entice people to join, and whether it delights the customer sufficiently to justify a long-term relationship. If there's product market fit, then small setbacks involving product mistakes and execution mishaps can be withstood.

Conclusion

Remember: you're in it for the long haul; set expectations accordingly. Expect some technology setbacks, partner conflicts, and pushback from colleagues and investors. If you have an existing successful business, you'll worry about cannibalizing your existing revenue. It's daunting to take this on. I'm asking operators like you to take a big risk, and I don't take that risk lightly. I truly believe that this path to recurring revenue and commitment to the long-term well-being of your customers leads to a stronger and more profitable business. Many organizations have found this to be a risk worth taking. I believe you will too.

What to Do Next

- Make sure you have a network of companies and advisors who've been there before and can help assess if the setbacks are "normal" and easily resolvable or are more serious and demand urgent action.
- Make a list of all the setbacks in this chapter. Rate the likelihood of each of them occurring in your organization. Are any of them starting to become visible?
- Review this list every month or two so you can act quickly on emerging setbacks.

11 Choose the Technology to Scale

Few Membership Economy startups have been as successful as online personal style company Stitch Fix. It launched in 2011, shipping boxes of hand-selected apparel to subscribers. Stitch Fix went public just six years later, in 2017, and was soon valued at $1.6 billion. As of February 2020, the company is valued at $2.4 billion. Subscribers like the clothes, and they usually fit. The company's success is attributed to personalized curation and customer perception that the clothes were picked just for them. But curation is only the tip of the iceberg. The accuracy and consistency of the Stitch Fix experience is remarkable. The company manages huge inventory, offers unprecedented personalization, and shipments take less than three days to arrive. And it accepts—even welcomes—returns and exchanges.

Most subscription companies make exciting promises but fail to deliver. End-to-end customer experience is an afterthought. They don't have adequate systems to manage payments, addresses, personalization, and supply chain. Stitch Fix is one of the

> ∞
>
> **"Back-end is the new front-end."**
>
> —Georg Richter, CEO of OceanX

few e-commerce companies for which this isn't the case, according to Georg Richter, the CEO of the all-in-one direct-to-consumer recurring revenue delivery platform OceanX.[1] Richter, who was COO of Guthy-Renker prior to launching OceanX, says the difference between profit and loss (success and failure) is in the back-end. He likes to tell his clients, "back-end is the new front-end." In other words, back-end systems are crucial in building the strong, loyal relationships the Membership Economy depends on.

In the scaling process, one of the biggest challenges for most subscription companies is implementing the technology and business processes needed. From initial acquisition to fulfillment of value, this challenge is complicated by three things: the plethora of vendor solutions, inexperienced technology buyers, and unfamiliar requirements.

A Crowded Technology Field

The technology tools available to subscription businesses today are vastly different than even five years ago. The availability of software-as-a-service (SaaS) allows more people to quickly and easily get into the recurring revenue business. Fuel x McKinsey, the consulting firm's startup-oriented company, valued the 2017 subscription ecommerce (subscription box, automated replenishment models, etc.) market at $20 billion, and predicted that Amazon.com's subscription revenue alone would grow by another $8 billion by 2020, bringing the total, conservatively speaking, to $28 billion.[2]

With many companies venturing into subscriptions, it's no wonder that the options for technology solutions keep growing. Abundant choices make it harder to pick the best solution for your business.*

Some subscription technology companies came out of the billing industry or are payment processors extending their capabilities. Others

---

* The "Paradox of Choice" is an idea developed by psychologist Barry Schwartz in his book *The Paradox of Choice* that even though we want more choices, we are unhappy when we have too many.

began in industries known for subscription models, like SaaS, publishing, consumer products, or streaming media. Many vendors are actually spinouts from industry pioneers, like OceanX, which emerged from direct-to-consumer subscription juggernaut Guthy-Renker, or Arc Publishing, created at the Washington Post. These vendors have deep vertical expertise in a particular industry but may lack the horizontal focus in understanding the functional discipline enough to ensure that their solutions are transferable to other industries. And some come to this market from adjacent fields such as customer support, digital community, marketing, or analytics, like digital media company Piano.io. Each of these vendors brings a unique set of competencies and experiences to their platforms. Some may be a better fit for you than others.

It can be confusing to determine the right combination of vendors, and who should have responsibility for which steps in your business processes. Here's one example of the potential for technology confusion. An organization might choose to generate subscription orders in at least four different places in the processing technology stack: as part of your e-commerce platform, in your order management system, in an enterprise resource planning (ERP) system, or as provided by your credit card processor. But when you talk to the vendors, they will all say they are the experts in subscriptions and that their platform should be at the core of your business processes. How do you choose where to place this mission critical function and whom to trust?

Inexperienced Buyers

The challenge is further exacerbated by the massive change in how companies evaluate and purchase technology solutions. Ten or 15 years ago, when a business unit needed a new technology solution, it would assign a technical business analyst to identify requirements. That business analyst would work with the internal technology organization to create an RFP (request for proposal) and manage the purchase process. With the rise of SaaS, technology became an operating expense, not a capital one.

Business owners now conduct buying cycles themselves, often without a business analyst or input from the IT department. There are some advantages to this. The technologies are easier to implement and require less technical expertise for onboarding. They're easy to try out in a small way before expanding.

But there's a downside, too. Most marketers and operators are not experts at developing business requirements for technology acquisitions or managing the purchase process. Many of them don't enjoy it, so they rush, often settling on the first solution they encounter. This is aggravated by CEOs pushing for speed to market, and quoting Mark Zuckerberg's "Move fast and break things" mantra reputed to be used by engineers at Facebook.*[3] Organizations should move fast, but not if things break. In fact, Zuckerberg has edited his mantra. Now it's "move fast with stable infra,"[4] and while it's less catchy, it's more useful.

According to Jane Wilkinson, former president of Institutional Investor and an expert on subscription models, "tech start-ups and retail businesses trying to transition to subscription-based models tend to be run by product- or tech-centric CEOs. They are employing mostly traditional marketing people, i.e., advertising, brand and creative led, rather than database and direct/subscription marketing people. Those marketing people don't tend to have a history of understanding customer lifetime value or the role of technology in subscription-based business infrastructures. In this ease-of-use SaaS world, companies large and small can quickly paint themselves into an architectural corner."[5]

---

* In April of 2014, Zuckerberg reworded his motto to the less sexy but more effective "Move fast with stable infra." "We used to have this famous mantra . . . and the idea here is that as developers, moving quickly is so important that we were even willing to tolerate a few bugs in order to do it," Zuckerberg said. "What we realized over time is that it wasn't helping us to move faster because we had to slow down to fix these bugs and it wasn't improving our speed."

Kathy Greenler Sexton, CEO and publisher of Subscription Insider, told me that the first vendor to respond to a potential customer is 50 percent more likely to close the sale than those that follow.[6] SaaS salespeople are generally highly experienced, well-compensated, and very good at going for the close. A naive business exec doesn't stand a chance.

What results is an odd tension. On one hand, the person responsible for scaling has a clear idea of what the business needs to be successful. They understand the importance of acquisition *and* retention metrics, flexibility to test different pricing and offers, and regional distinctions in regulation and customs. They want sophisticated analytical tools to help establish the right dashboard. And they have a vision of what the business will look like.

On the other hand, the business owner may underestimate the importance of integrating their technology tools with the organization's broader corporate technology stack. Because this might be the first, or only, time that they lead a major tech implementation, they don't have any template to work from. For example, their IT department may be working toward "global inventory visibility," or a BOPIS (buy online, pick up in store) strategy whereby subscriptions should be incorporated into a bigger multichannel picture. But if the business owner hands the whole project over to the tech organization, they run the risk of losing momentum and not getting the membership features they need.

Unfamiliar Requirements

Determining which features to prioritize is already difficult for the business team because subscription models are uncharted waters for many organizations. Some purchasers neglect key requirements because they haven't thought of them yet or haven't reached the right level of maturity to need them.

Sexton told me that when she asks a room full of subscription professionals, both marketers and payment experts, whether they track and analyze customer lifetime value (CLV) by source or timing of acquisition, very few do, although nearly all will claim CLV is among the most important metrics. As sophisticated as the industry has grown since I wrote *The Membership Economy*, there's still so much room for companies to incorporate best practices. In many cases, a customer acquired through a referral channel might have a CLV that is six times the lifetime value of an affiliate marketing program. If you're not measuring CLV, you'd miss this important fact.

Emerging requirements are less of an issue if the subscription company continues to evolve and improve its technology footprint.

> In an ideal world, organizations would reevaluate the technology stack for its membership economy business every year.

In an ideal world, organizations would reevaluate the technology stack for their membership economy business every year, stepping back to see what they'd be buying if they were just starting in subscriptions. Buying software for membership economy businesses is like decorating your house—the minute you're done, you realize all the things you'd do differently. And then, before you know it, everything that was cutting edge becomes dated. Some features are big and hard to change once you've committed, like your billing system, while others are easier to swap out, like your A/B testing technology. At the same time, it's easy to let the project balloon out of control. As Michael La Guardia, SVP digital product at Under Armour, told me, "beware the tyranny of secondary goals."[7] When you're creating requirements for your project, stay focused on what you absolutely need to launch, rather than incorporating too many "nice to haves."

Many subscription companies are using the technology equivalent of a horse and buggy to drive their businesses. Unless they proactively benchmark themselves or ask new hires for input, they don't recognize that they're falling behind. This is especially true if retention is high—it gives them the illusion that their business is strong. But you always need to balance acquisition and retention.

Selecting technology is not a fundamental skill of every business-person, but it's time to hone your expertise and play an active role in this area. You don't need to be an engineer or know how to code. You do need to identify opportunities to employ emerging tech solutions to strengthen your business, and to assess when and how much to invest.

Product marketers use "product requirements" documents to communicate to their engineers what the product capacities need to be, and why. As you do your rollout, create your own user requirements document to explain what your technology needs to do to support your new processes. For example, even if you're not familiar with the rising discipline of customer success, you probably have requirements like tracking how customers engage with products after purchase. Which articles do they click on, and how long do they stay? Many companies, including the Financial Times,[8] track recency, frequency, and depth (volume or breadth of articles, or even total time spent) of visits. You might also want to get proactive about retaining customers—what behavior do they exhibit before canceling; what remedial actions could you take to prevent the churn? Once you know how to handle retention, you can seek vendors who do those things.

Tips for Selecting Your Tech

Before you reach out, look inward. Scott Brinker's "Martech Landscape" research suggests there are hundreds of technology solutions that support deeper customer relationships.[9] Rather than getting familiar with all of the vendors, first identify your *objectives*. Understand what you're trying to accomplish in your business. Answer questions like the following before you scope your requirements:

- Who's your ideal buyer, and what's the forever promise?
- What will your customer need to be able to do? Today? Tomorrow?
- What will you track to understand how you're doing and where the emerging problems are?

- Can you break it out by benefits? By features?
- Is it worthwhile talking to other subscription business owners who have recently gone through this process?
- What might trigger sign-up? What hooks customers for life?
- What is the role of freemium and free trials, and are they justified by the CLV?

Consider every step of the customer experience, and every step of your internal business process. Kim Terry, of Subscription Systems LLC, and an expert on technology issues relating to recurring revenue business models, reminds his clients that every step of the process from awareness through purchase through fulfillment can impact the business's health and profitability. There are a million details to get right, from making sure that prospects aren't repeatedly taking advantage of free trials, to managing the complexity of different types of orders, to credit processing issues, to managing refunds. Terry explains that managing a subscription business is "like managing a logging operation. The river of orders needs to float downstream smoothly, or revenue and costs are negatively impacted."[10]

Envision the kinds of dashboards you might need to make strategic decisions over time. Beware of chasing micro-improvements without a larger strategy. For example, many news organizations have taken a growth-hacker approach to building reader engagement, assuming that clicks are a good proxy for reader interest. But clicks are only an indicator of title quality, not good indicators of what people will read, and certainly not what people will pay for. I might click on a sensational link like "5 things you need to know about Kim Kardashian's morning routine" but may not read the article. If there's a paywall, blocking between me and that article, I'm going to move on and click "Where Beyoncé goes on vacation."

If you focus on optimizing individual design elements—learning that people click more on green than blue links and prefer titles starting with "how" over "why"—you might get some improvements, but you're not developing insights that align with your value. For example, if you are a skin care company, you don't necessarily get to know your customer's needs through A/B testing alone. You have to go back to the forever transaction. Improving things like box size and bonus gifts without taking a step back and saying "if the goal is to have the best skin, gifts generally are not really aligned and that money is better spent on a gift that improves skin." Understand your budget. You might not know what the right budget is, so maybe a looser definition is appropriate, like "the least expensive solution that solves xyz problems but is still commercially justifiable."

You need a single view of the customer, no matter how many different services there are and how many different individuals use them. Customer privacy and data security are essential, even if you don't operate in markets with strong privacy regulations, like the EU's General Data Protection Regulation (GDPR). The more information you gather about customers, the greater your responsibility to protect it. A forever transaction is built on trust; invest in robust cybersecurity measures.

Be honest about how technologically sophisticated you are as the buyer and how adept your team will be as users. Think about how specialized a solution you need. There are technology solutions optimized for every industry as well as for every functional area, and point solutions that solve a particular problem as well as "all in one" technologies that need customization but provide an integrated solution.

With a firm grasp of your internal needs, you can look outward to understand your vendor options. Or consider employing some outside assistance. If you don't feel confident about your business strategy, hold off on the major tech investment.

One of the most common scaling problems arises when organizations start by looking at products, without mapping out the bigger requirements first. It's kind of like going grocery shopping when you're hungry, without a list. If you start with the end in mind, you'll be ahead of the game. It's wise to plan for your entire subscription architecture, even if you're not implementing it all up front. You have demand generation websites and social media, order capture, order processing, subscription generation, customer financials, business analytics, customer support, business accounting, and, if you ship physical products, warehouse and fulfillment. Many of these areas can be combined when you are small, then broken out into more sophisticated individual components as your company grows. Choose wisely, then, as you grow, swap in full-featured products that work with the rest of your architecture. Make sure today's choices are built with API functionality and come with a list of supported third-party integrations. If you take this path, you want vendors who are committed to scalable growth.

With each vendor you consider, ask about the organization's roots. What industry do its executives come from? Are they media types? Enterprise software veterans? The leaders vendors choose have huge implications for their business direction, their biases, and potentially their blind spots. You might gain benefits from a vendor who knows your industry, but there's a risk of bias toward an old-fashioned way of looking at your space. Companies that have worked with a SaaS company doing multiyear global contracts will have different requirements than a consumer app, utility company, or streaming service. Talk to references and notice the customer logos on vendors' websites to see if they have experience working with customers like you.

Choosing and implementing your technology is not easy. The best advice I can give you is to expect bumps and remember that the exercise of reevaluating your technology is valuable no matter what structure your business takes. Remember in Chapter 5 when we discussed Hagerty's Eric Okerstrom who helped create Drivers Club? He found that through their process, "We were forced to confront 'the brutal truth' of where we were technologically versus where we needed to be. Although sometimes painful—I think this is the 'silver lining' to the challenges we've faced. We're maturing as a business overall and setting ourselves up for more growth and success."[11]

What to Do Next

- If you have no budget and need to make do with existing infrastructure for now, determine which processes are most critical to delivering on your forever promise. Find manual ways to manage these processes. The advantage to this approach is that it can be easier and less costly to experiment this way—and by the time you are ready to invest in technology, you'll be very clear about your requirements.
- If you are just getting started or planning a major tech investment, make sure to start with your strategic requirements. Keep it as simple as possible and protect the project from getting "hijacked" into a much bigger project.
- If you are midway through a tech project and want to optimize it from wherever you are, take a step back, and look at your strategic requirements. You might be able to trim your project and get it refocused on what's needed to scale. You don't need to do it all at once—it's going to be an iterative, evolving project.

12 Create and Fine-Tune Your Pricing Strategy

People ask me more questions about pricing than just about any other topic, although I don't see pricing as the most important issue when building a membership model. Much more critical is a clear forever promise that justifies recurring payments and the sharing of information by your customer. It's more important that you understand product-market fit and determine whether your customers are willing to pay for the solution you provide.

You might be eager to advance to the efficient frontier of pricing, the point at which you're charging exactly what your members are willing to pay, no more, no less. But most organizations struggle to find sensible pricing that creates a win/win for the company and the customer. I believe pricing/packaging options can work but that the trickier your pricing, the more complex your communications become. Complicated communications erode your customers' trust, especially in the early phase of the relationship. Over time, your organization may create more personalized and sophisticated offers to overcome pricing limitations for loyal customers, but clarity should always be a priority.

I travel a lot and so I subscribe to The Points Guy. He's built a business helping flyers get the best prices and greatest value from airline loyalty points. He helps consumers understand the pricing so they can get a fair deal. Airline pricing is so complex, you need to be an expert; you can't trust the airlines to price fairly. If you don't do your research, you'll overpay.

Airlines have sophisticated algorithms to maximize revenue, using information about specific customers, routes, and flights. But they pay a price in lack of trust. A 2018 travel survey by software company Boxever found that consumers want pricing transparency and that 57 percent of them said they will dump an airline over hidden fees.[1]

Pricing isn't the only thing, but it is important. Once you move away from a la carte pricing and toward a simpler recurring model, you need to understand consumer behavior, competitive forces, and your own costs really well. Pricing that's simple for customers to understand isn't necessarily simple for you to create.

Getting Started with Pricing

When first launching your offer, you face a seemingly infinite number of pricing options. Of course, you can continue to price by transactions, even if you're working toward a more formal and ongoing relationship.

> With transactional pricing, each purchase decision requires effort and mindshare for the customer, and creates risk for the organization that the customer will choose *not* to conduct the transaction.

For example, while Uber has introduced subscription pricing, initially they only charged by the trip, even though they expected customers to return repeatedly. Launching with a transactional model can feel less risky than moving to subscription pricing because each customer is paying as they go for what they use. With transactional pricing, each purchase decision requires effort and mindshare for the customer, and creates risk for the organization that the customer will choose *not* to conduct the transaction.

Subscription pricing enjoys tremendous popularity because once someone subscribes, automatic payments continue until they cancel. But to price subscriptions, you almost always have some people getting more or less value (and maybe driving greater or lower costs of goods sold). Companies fear their least profitable subscribers will tank the business or their most profitable subscribers will find the offer unappealing and cancel. Some companies offer subscription *and* a la carte pricing, with dozens of price points and options for customers and subscribers. This is intended to give everyone the ideal offer, but in reality, it's just confusing.

I explained in *The Membership Economy* how to set a beta price and adjust it based on behavior.[2] Even with variable costs, this is possible— Netflix launched with variable shipping costs for three DVDs out at a time. Most buffets in Vegas charge the same price whether you eat a lot or a little, whether you prefer oysters or pasta. It's important to start simple and leave room for flexibility. Also, set expectations early that this is launch pricing and may change.

Five Advanced Pricing Strategies to Consider as You Grow

If you've been operating for a while, you may want to change your pricing to better fit what you've learned about customer behavior and your own costs. Or you might want to add options for target segments of customers whose needs are not well met by the way you currently package value. Here are some strategies to consider.

Strategy 1: Keep Control of Diagnosis and Prescription as You Grow

When you're working with prospects and customers, it's helpful to assume the role of physician.

If you went to a heart surgeon and said, "I'm having trouble breathing. It's a heart attack. Quick, give me a triple bypass so I can successfully run a marathon next month," the surgeon would kick you out of the office, laugh, or both.

That's because the patient shouldn't diagnose (it's a heart attack) or prescribe (give me a triple bypass). The patient is qualified to describe the symptoms (I'm having trouble breathing) and the desired outcome (run the marathon). An honest physician would caution that the desired outcome isn't likely. Having your pricing and packaging dictated by a prospect is similar. The prospect can tell you their goals and challenges, but it's up to you to determine how to deliver.

I'm proposing what "solution selling"*" experts have been teaching for years. You're not selling widgets or over-the-counter meds. You're selling a solution to the customer's *ongoing* problem. Over time, you will continue to add and adapt that solution to meet the customer's evolving needs and to take advantage of the best resources in a changing environment and ecosystem.

Even if the customer thinks they need only one feature, if you know they need multiple features to get the results they want, it's your obligation to tell them.

Strategy 2: Incorporate "Free" Strategically

If you offer anything for free, you need to know why and have a quantifiable rationale. For example, you might offer something for free for marketing or sales purposes. You might use a free offer for testing and learning (kind of marketing again, but also product/operations). Make sure that you are getting results. Giving something away for free, even if there's no "variable cost," comes with an opportunity cost.

> If you offer free anything, you need to know why and have a quantifiable rationale.

If you're un-strategically giving things away, you're teaching the market that there are deals to be had and

---

* "Solution selling" is a commonly used term to describe a sales methodology that focuses on solving the customer's problem, rather than on the product being sold.

possibly lowering the perception of your offering's value. You could find yourself, as many "freemium" models do, in a situation where the free version is "good enough" for most customers. They would have been willing to pay but didn't have to.

Many companies remove essential service from free versions. They might offer product sandboxes or freemium subscriptions to "lite" products without onboarding and support necessary for the offering to shine. They might lose subscribers who would have been great customers.

> Freemium is access to a limited set of features forever, for free. To be a true freemium offer, it needs to be both of those things— free and forever.

You need to be strategic, whether you offer "free trials" or a freemium model (which means some subscribers get free value forever while others pay a premium for more features, service, or volume), or your full subscription for free to influencers and leaders in your market.

A free trial is a taste of something delicious. Use a free trial when your prospect doesn't understand what your product tastes like, or if your customer doesn't believe your promise and needs to experience the wow for themselves. Don't skimp on the quality of a free trial; but leave them hungry for more.

Let's say your customer knows what your product tastes like, but isn't sure they'll use it enough to justify subscribing. You won't get their business through a free trial and offering one to them is a waste of money and resources.

This customer needs a freemium option. Freemium is access to a limited set of features forever, for free. To be a true freemium offer, it needs to be both of those things—free and forever.

The job of this freemium option is to change the customer's behavior . . . to get them so engaged with your product that they realize they're better off paying for the premium version. This is where you might offer a stripped-down version without support. Or you might limit the volume of usage—number of users, number of sessions, amount of storage. For example, SurveyMonkey's freemium offer, which they call "Basic," allows unlimited surveys of 10 questions or less and no personalized support. Their Standard Program offers unlimited questions, but limited responses, and customer support via email.

Many businesses such as marketplaces or communities use freemium to build membership because members attract the paying subscribers.

Someone could get great value from the freemium option forever, if all they use it for is a quick customer satisfaction survey. But it's easy to see how an active market researcher might quickly crave longer surveys or want to talk with someone about maximizing product features. In a business-to-business (B2B) organization, price is often not the biggest hurdle—changing behavior and adopting the new product is. By letting the surveyor "play with" the freemium option, SurveyMonkey demonstrates what the app can do, and slowly makes the app integral to how that person does her job.

Freemium models do a couple of other things for your business model. Even if a SurveyMonkey freemium user never upgrades to the premium version, someone receiving a survey *from* that person might become a paid subscriber. In other words, freemium can drive organic viral growth. This is especially important if your product connects your target buyers—for example, billing software sent to people who also have billing needs.

Many businesses such as marketplaces or communities use freemium to build membership because members attract the paying subscribers. Some companies that build products for software developers know that their products need to be familiar to all software developers, not just the ones who pay for them and routinely use them.

A final thought about free: companies sometimes give away subscriptions to influencers. These may be well-known professionals who blog or create industry insider content, or individuals inside large companies. There are times to give away subscriptions, but it's important to understand *why* you're doing it, especially in B2B, where money is rarely the hurdle preventing purchase. Sometimes higher usage is driven by charging for the product instead of giving it away. Resist the short-term desire to add another customer by focusing on long-term engagement and growth. That decision will lead to a healthier business model.

If you haven't experimented with "free" as part of your business model, I encourage you to do it. It's an easy exercise to test.

Start by listing all the ways you might use free—free trial, free-mium, free for influencers. How could you structure these offerings? Who would they target? What behavior would they drive? Share your list with the most creative and experienced strategists in your organization—maybe even get it on the leadership team's next meeting for a 15-minute brainstorm. It's useful to involve leadership because they're often the people throwing out ideas about strategic use of free at the most inopportune times.

Evaluate the cost and benefit of each idea on your list. Are these lead generation strategies, or awareness strategies? What problem are they solving and for whom?

From there, if you have any promising options, map out a small test (ping me and I'll try to help). If you don't have any promising options, that's good too; you can quickly shut down well-intentioned but distracting suggestions.

Strategy 3: Price for Use Cases, Not One-Off Requests

Many subscription billing companies make it possible to structure your subscription business flexibly. You can offer custom pricing for each subscriber, or have an infinite number of SKUs, or price on factors including time lapse, usage, number of users, or volume . . . you get the idea. The options are truly limitless.

Subscription billing platforms impose few limits to creative and responsive pricing. There are many good reasons to customize pricing. You might have third-party obligations—partners or resellers who receive a share of revenue or blanket pricing discounts, each with slightly different structures. You might encounter different legal constraints or pricing norms in different regions and countries. Or you might bid for government contracts with their sometimes arbitrary requirements. You might want to give subscribers the ability to determine what they wish to pay, as explored in Richard Reisman's book, *FairPay: Adaptively Win-Win Customer Relationships.*[3]

Flexibility can be valuable. You'll be grateful many times to be able to design digital processes via your platform that reflect your complex business environments. That doesn't mean you have to use *all* the features *all* the time. Your pricing features have to follow your pricing logic. And with flexibility comes complexity, which could make other parts of your business harder, like forecasting future revenue.

I have a client in the font business, Monotype. This company makes it easy for professional designers to access thousands of fonts. And most professional designers pay (or their companies pay) to have access to this broad resource. It doesn't mean the designers use every font for every project. They may never use most of the fonts. They use discretion, often just one or two fonts at a time, and make sure that they're complementary, focusing on the primary objective of communication.

The same should be true of how you employ pricing. Flexibility is a tool to address the demands of organizational complexity over time at the macro level and the demands of evolving customer needs on the micro level. Be disciplined with your pricing to ensure it always supports your long-term business model.

Here are some good reasons to increase your pricing options:

- You've evaluated your sales and onboarding process and there's a step missing for which you need to create a pricing option.
- You have multiple discrete functions in your product, many of which are irrelevant or confusing to certain customer segments. You don't want to force your customers to buy more than they need.
- Something's not working quite right in your current pricing and you want to experiment.
- You want to offer a free trial.
- You're working with a broad range of customers with a variety of need states, and your pricing isn't flexible enough to reflect the massive difference in value created.

One great reason to add to your pricing options is to make a subscription model available in the first place. If you're moving from a transactional model to a subscription, you might want to offer both for a while, while you're experimenting. And you might find that one works great in certain situations but the other is still needed.

It's your job to understand how customers can get the greatest value from your products and services. Then you are morally obligated (in my opinion) to price in the space where your best interest and the customer's best interest are maximized.

A good approach is to price for use cases. Many companies need to reconsider how they bundle (or unbundle) ongoing services with single-use add-ons.

Start by identifying a customer with an unmet need and then determine if there's a group of people with similar issues. Don't create a new pricing model for each customer. Mass customization of pricing can make it hard to improve the product. The more varied the need states of your customers, and the more offers you have, the harder it will be to satisfy all of them well.

> **Pricing is the servant, not the master. Strategy is in charge.**

Sometimes what looks like diversity of usage all comes out in the wash. For example, if you're concerned that some customers use your services more heavily than others, determine whether the lightest users are still getting good value from the current pricing before you lower that pricing. A hungry football player at the buffet pays the same as the slender gymnast. Some items are far more expensive than others (think of the gym members stretching out on a mat vs the ones using the pool or the Pilates equipment). Understand how everyone is using the offering—it might all come out in the wash. Track engagement before jumping to conclusions about pricing.

If every customer has different needs and pricing how do you optimize your road map? Structure your customer success team? It becomes hard to know where the organization is going if you do no pruning of your customer tree. Pricing is the servant, not the master. Strategy is in charge.

Strategy 4: Use Engagement Data to Develop Pricing Extensions

Customer engagement data is critical in understanding how to price.

Many subscription and membership companies have a "retention" team, and a retention communication drip in advance of renewal, perhaps a notice that the next shipment is being sent in 48 hours or text reminder that the next payment date is coming up. Many organizations have a "save" program to deploy when someone calls to cancel, in hopes of saving them. Those tactics are the most basic tools. More sophisticated organizations track behavior, and communicate with subscribers, from the beginning. They understand how customers onboard, how they feel about unboxing their products, how they test new software features or explore the content catalog. They quickly recognize whether a new subscriber is likely to churn. In some cases, the subscriber is the primary beneficiary, and immediately begins using the subscription as expected. Other times, the subscriber is acting on behalf of others, like children or work colleagues, and you will need to sell the beneficiaries on using the services which someone else paid for. Be prepared to have to "resell" some product users on the value of your offering that you may have already sold the buyers on.

One of the huge advantages of digital subscriptions and membership models is how much you know about how people engage with your product.

You might notice heavier usage among certain cohorts or during certain seasons, triggering a higher value option. Light usage might trigger a commensurately less expensive version. Start with communicating what's available and acknowledging usage. You might need a new price point to meet their needs. But don't wait until renewal time to have these conversations. Seek to understand the engagement data early on, both to maximize renewal and to gain insights for optimal pricing going forward.

One of the huge advantages of digital subscriptions and membership models is how much you can learn about how people engage with your product. This should provide you with insight relative to pricing, product road map, communication, and support. Decisions on all of these topics should be integrated and made with the long-term customer relationship at the center.

Evaluate three types of engagement data to make forward-looking decisions:

- **Recency:** When was the last time that the customer logged in?
- **Frequency:** How frequently do they engage?
- **Depth:** When they log in, how many features do they use and for how long?

Each of these types of engagement data can inform future pricing considerations.

If there's an issue with *recency*, meaning that usage tails off after early enthusiasm wanes, consider charging full price for the first month and offering a second month free if they've successfully onboarded. This strategy applies whether your product is software, content, services, or a physical product like clothing or makeup. Does the customer unbox on day one, or does the box sit in the front hall for a few days because they dread opening it and feel guilty about the last shipment they've never used?

If there's an issue with *frequency*, meaning that users aren't engaging with the product as often as you had expected, there could be two different reasons, each with different implications for pricing. First, they're not using the product as intended. For example, the product is optimized for daily use but the customer is only logging in every few days. In this case, keep the same pricing, but change the onboarding to encourage people to change their behavior. On the other hand, maybe they're not using the product every day because they don't need it every day. A lighter pricing model is appropriate for subscribers who have a lighter use case.

If the problem is *depth* of usage, such as how many features the customer uses or how long they spend each time the use it, then you need to figure out if the lighter usage is due to misuse (i.e., the customer didn't know the features were available but could definitely benefit from using them) or lack of need. In the former case, you have a communications issue. In the latter, it might be a pricing problem.

Remember, all departments touch pricing, so check to see what they're learning about how the customer is engaging with you. Accounting can raise a flag if you're just over the "expense" maximum, and your pricing structure requires a rigorous approval process. That could be a good reason to lower pricing. Or marketing might have ascertained how your pricing structure prevents a particular group from signing up and have insight about removing the friction. Sales will be more than happy to point out all the price-driven reasons that they're not hitting their quota!

> ∞
>
> **Keep the customer front and center. When you're evaluating your pricing, think about how your "best customers" use your product, and how to price to support proper usage and optimal benefits.**

Keep the customer front and center. When you're evaluating your pricing, think about how your "best customers" use your product, and how to price to support proper usage and optimal benefits. The *Financial Times* has added a new metric to more closely track successful outcomes for readers, "quality reads" which refers to "the percentage of page views where the reader has read at least half of the article, estimated by time on page, scroll depth, and what it knows about how subscribers interact with similar content."[4] This new metric helps them understand both which articles (and not just clickbait titles) were most valued by subscribers as well as which subscribers engaged with each article in a meaningful way.

Strategy 5: Make Sure Your Pricing Is Easy for Customers to Understand

I use a rule borrowed from Albert Einstein with all my clients: "Keep your pricing as simple as possible, but no simpler." What does this mean? The more complex the pricing, the less customers trust it. The more they have to become experts on your pricing, the more they're going to look for ways you're not being fair.

You may have reasons for complex pricing. Customers come in all shapes and sizes. They need different features or have different budgets. Some companies might have many individuals using the product and need a dashboard to track and manage usage, while others might have a single person. All of these variables drive your costs and also can drive value for your subscribers.

Even if it's complicated for you to manage, make sure you can explain the pricing in a simple, intuitive way. Ideally, you can convey how you price in three steps or fewer:

- **Step 1:** Choose your features (functionality, service, support, customization).
- **Step 2:** Choose your size (how many people, how many sites, how much storage etc.).
- **Step 3:** Choose the duration (monthly, annually, multi-year).

Blending features and providing the customer with exactly what she wants may be challenging, requiring you to jump through all kinds of legal and accounting hoops and potentially a new billing platform. But for customers it should be straightforward. They should know how the pricing works and why they paid what they did.

Beware of promotions. Offering end-of-quarter discounts or new-feature bundles can make you a hero today, but you'll pay for it tomorrow. This kind of revenue won't be sustainable—people who are making buying decisions on price may not stay with you for the right reasons. You're also educating your customers to wait for the sales and your company will quickly become addicted to sales. You'll be running a hamster wheel of constant promotions, distracting attention from the subscribers you already have.

When you're just starting out with pricing, it's enough to just get customers to sign up. After all, your fixed costs are mostly behind you and you're eager to demonstrate that you have referenceable customers. But as you grow, it's critical to dig into the details about how your subscribers use your product, what holds the prospects back from buying, and how to maximize customer lifetime value (CLV).

What to Do Next

* Take time to build a thoughtful and relevant pricing structure for your business. Look at competitors, assess value created by your offer, and consider your best customers' ability to pay, so you can triangulate pricing that makes sense.
* Understand the value you're creating.
* Taking the perspective of your best customers, do the math and see if your offering's value justifies the pricing.
* Get honest feedback on the pricing structure. Remember that the more complex your pricing structure, the less your customers will trust you—keep it clear enough for them to understand.

13 Essential Metrics for Long-Term Relationships

The metrics you use to track success in a forever transaction differs from those used in a transactional model. You have more data to track, which can help you quickly determine which lever to pull to strengthen your business. But in order to do that effectively, you need to understand the metrics that underpin your subscription model and make sure that your scorecard incorporates the relationship between the various metrics.

How Netflix Taught a New Approach to Metrics

One of Netflix's biggest challenges early on was educating stakeholders on the metrics to use to evaluate the company's financial health. From the beginning, Netflix has been a data-driven company. It knows which numbers to track to ensure it hits its short-term numbers *and* will succeed in the long term. Netflix recognized that the single biggest driver of success would be retention. Acquisition of new customers came with a two-week free trial, which had real variable costs. If a customer signed up for the free trial and then canceled before the first paid period, or even after just a period or two, the company lost money. It wasn't enough to acquire customers; Netflix had to keep the customer, or "subscriber," long enough to cover the trial as well as the cost to serve on an ongoing basis.

Additionally, Netflix perceived that engagement was a useful leading indicator of churn. People didn't use the service much in the weeks leading up to a cancellation, like they stop going to the gym weeks or months before they cancel their membership. It's partially inertia, and partially the aspirational belief (hope) they would use the service more in the future. Months two, three, and beyond were more profitable than the first month. Keeping an existing customer another month was better than attracting a new customer for a month.

At the time of the Netflix IPO, few public companies depended on digital subscriptions. HBO had a subscription model but went through intermediaries. Telecommunications organizations often had complex contracts that locked customers in, something Netflix has avoided. Newspaper subscriptions were mostly print, and publishers had limited data. As a result, Netflix was charting new territory and had to teach their investors which data would be most important. Netflix had lots of data and knew that its low and predictable monthly churn, combined with its carefully managed cost of acquisition, told a compelling story. But to understand the story, people needed to speak the language of subscription metrics.

Netflix worried as much about retention as it did acquisition, and it tracked trends across cohorts of new customers. Today, the metrics Netflix popularized are standard in businesses across many industries that use a subscription pricing model. Interestingly though, Netflix is coy about reporting "churn", perhaps an indicator of how valuable a metric it is.[1] From news to entertainment, and from hardware to software, companies that have ongoing formal relationships with their customers are moving away from the big-game hunting and an obsession with customer counts and transactions. Instead, they turn to the more measured, farming-like approach of a subscription.

Why Metrics Matter for Forever Relationships

Metrics always matter in business, but they matter more when you're trying to build a long-term relationship. In a traditional transactional business, once the customer buys something, that person is released back into the bigger pool of prospects, to be hunted down and released again and again. When you're building a forever transaction, the real opportunity to drive value happens after the first financial exchange. The lifetime value of any customer (customer lifetime value, or CLV) tracks how much that customer spends in the long term and it varies by customer. In other words, not all initial transactions are equal because some people leave right after that initial transaction, while others stay and even might sign up for more.

Metrics always matter in business, but they matter more when you're trying to build a long-term relationship.

Many investors are mystified by this membership or subscription model because they're too focused on acquisition. They assume that future revenue equals monthly recurring revenue multiplied by the number of new customers, without accounting for changes in retention over a customer life cycle. In most subscription businesses, the first month for a new subscriber has higher churn than later months, probably because the subscriber is still trying to decide whether or not to make the subscription a habit. If a company has mostly brand-new subscribers, the value of the cohort is lower than if most of the subscribers have been around a few months. Oversimplifying subscription metrics can be a costly mistake.

Oversimplifying subscription metrics can be a costly mistake.

Key Metrics and How to Use Them

As you shift to a forever transaction, some of the metrics that help the most are the same that you've probably used in other, more transaction-oriented businesses. There are also a few that you may not have used before. The most important thing to know about these metrics is how to use them in concert. Let's first review each metric and then look at how they work together. Although individually useful, no single metric stands on its own.

Customer Acquisition Cost (CAC)

Customer acquisition cost (sometimes called cost per acquisition, or CPA) is the amount the company spends to acquire a new customer—marketing/ad cost plus any direct trial expenses. Some organizations don't incorporate those direct trial expenses and call them part of cost of goods sold (COGS), which can hide the actual cost of bringing on a new subscriber. CAC can be measured by channel or campaign and can also be averaged. It's important because once you find a predictable way to acquire customers, and you know how much each customer is worth (see CLV, below), you can build a "marketing machine" to predictably grow revenue and profitability. People often ask for a specific CAC benchmark—should a new customer cost three euros? Or 50? It depends on the business, and the customer lifetime value. Don't let anyone tell you there's an arbitrary benchmark. It's like asking what's a good price for a restaurant meal, or a pair of shoes—it depends. CAC is useful for trends over time, and also when compared to the customer lifetime value it drives.

Customer Lifetime Value (CLV) and Expected CLV

Customer lifetime value is the total amount of revenue generated by a customer over time. This metric is important because not all customers are equally valuable. For example, let's say you and I both subscribe to LinkedIn Learning, but you're committed to professional development and I just need to learn how to use Microsoft Excel. I might cancel in the first month after binge-watching all of its Excel-oriented content. You might subscribe for years, watching two or three courses each month.

A customer like you, who values lifelong learning, is more valuable than one like me, who has a time-sensitive and narrow need. Knowing this might give LinkedIn a way to estimate "expected CLV" based on behavior in the first week of trial—people who access multiple courses are more valuable than those who just dive into one course. LinkedIn might choose marketing messages about learning rather than about any specific course. It might decide not to offer a complete course during a free trial so that people like me can't game the system. But CLV isn't, by itself, a barometer of business health. Even if CLV is high, without knowing how much it costs to acquire that customer or how many customers you have, it's hard to know how the business is doing.

CLV/CAC Ratio

If you know the cost to acquire a new customer and the value of that customer, you can develop a ratio that predicts your return on investment (ROI). Companies that have a strong CLV/CAC ratio can comfortably "add gasoline to the fire" and grow their business. They are also more attractive to investors who see less risk. This metric is not an obvious one, and it is one that would benefit from more widespread use. Many investors consider a CLV/CAC ratio of three to one to be attractive. That is, if it costs $30 to acquire a new customer and that customer is worth $90, that's a good investment.

> **Even if CLV is high, without knowing how much it costs to acquire that customer or how many customers you have, it's hard to know how the business is doing.**

Net Promoter System (NPS) Score

Fred Reichheld of Bain & Co. popularized the concept of NPS scores in his bestselling book *The Ultimate Question* from Harvard Business School Press.[2] The idea is that if you have more customers who would recommend your business than those who would badmouth your business, you have a healthy business. Here's how to calculate NPS score. Ask subscribers this question: "On a scale of 0–10, how likely is it that you would recommend this to your friends, family, or business associates?" Customers that give you a 6 or below are Detractors, those with a score of 7 or 8 are called Passives, and those with a 9 or 10 are Promoters.

Calculate what percentage of subscribers are Promoters and Detractors. Then subtract the percentage of Detractors from the percentage of Promoters.

This metric is particularly important in subscription businesses where companies depend on an ongoing relationship with their customers and, in many cases, an element of community or network effect. However, some businesses that have excellent NPS scores may have artificially rigged the score. I recently called a customer service hotline, and toward the end of my call, the rep told me I'd be receiving a survey and he sincerely hoped I'd give them a 10 out of 10. Those scores would not be a fair measure of business health.

Churn and Churn Drivers

Churn is the percentage of customers who leave in a given period. Churn rate is equal to the number of customers who canceled divided by the total customers at the start of the month. Most companies don't spend enough time understanding churn. Why do customers leave, and what causes them to go? It's important to know whether the churn percent is based on monthly churn or annual churn—an impressive monthly retention of 93 percent (7 percent churn) still means you're losing more than 50 percent of your subscribers annually.

> Generally, churn is highest in a subscriber's first few months, so businesses that are growing fast might have higher churn than a stagnant one—counterintuitive, but important to note.

Once you know the churn number, it's important to segment the drivers of churn. For example, if people churn at the end of the free trial (before they are charged), they might have never intended to subscribe, which is different than people not converting because they're disappointed by the experience. One of my clients had a streaming subscription that lost a lot of people during the free trial because its streaming technology wasn't reliable. That requires a product fix. In contrast, a software-as-a-service (SaaS) client found that its subscribers felt the service was too hard to implement—a problem fixed with better communication up front about how to use the service.

Some drivers of churn are passive, like when a credit card expires and the customer never gets around to entering the new one. Others are active, like when the customer calls to cancel because she doesn't value (or use) the subscription enough. And some drivers of churn are acceptable (Table 13.1). If I retire, I probably don't need a career coach anymore. If I move away, maybe I should cancel my local gym membership. Passive churn can often be fixed with an outsourced solution—there are many software services that help with payment issues. Active churn usually requires either a product fix or a targeting/communication fix. And acceptable churn is, well, acceptable—one less thing to worry about.

While generally all businesses want low churn, some businesses are so focused on churn that they stop acquiring new subscribers. Generally, churn is highest in a subscriber's first few months, so businesses that are growing fast might have higher churn than a stagnant one—counterintuitive, but important to note.

TABLE 13.1 Churn

	Active Churn	**Passive Churn**
Unacceptable Churn	The subscription doesn't work as promised The subscription isn't what I expected	My card expired
Acceptable Churn	I moved away I don't need the subscription anymore I used up all of the value in the subscription	None

Average Revenue Per User (ARPU) and Average Revenue Per Account (ARPA)

To calculate average revenue per user, or ARPU, divide total monthly recurring revenue by total users of the service. There is a similar metric,

ARPA, for average revenue per account. This metric assesses the expected value to the monthly recurring revenue (MRR, see below) of each additional subscriber. Over time, it can be a useful tool to determine changes in spending behavior among customers—for example, if more people choose a higher or lower tier of membership. As with any "average" measurement, this metric is useful, but it might mask unique segments that behave very differently from one another.

Monthly Recurring Revenue (MRR) and Annual Recurring Revenue (ARR)

To find MRR, or monthly recurring revenue, add total billings from existing subscribers in a given month to the first month payments from new customers. ARR is calculated similarly but for a given year. Each year, of course, this number is different, although the average revenue per user might stay relatively constant. You can use MRR and ARR to track healthy growth and profitability.

Many investors focus too much on recurring revenue without considering whether growth in MRR is a function of high new customer acquisition (an often expensive tactic) offsetting high churn. Don't make their mistake. Instead, make sure to look at multiple metrics so you can ensure that you're both attracting new subscribers and retaining, and even extending, the existing ones.

Trial Conversion Rate

Most subscription businesses experiment with trial offers. A free trial is a small taste of a product or experience. You need a trial if your prospects are reluctant to just sign up because they don't understand what your product is, or they don't believe it can do what you say it does. A free trial is about understanding and credibility.

Yet many companies offer trials that can be used multiple times, or that provide so much value that the customer doesn't need to pay for the subscription at all. For example, many news organizations offer 10 articles a month free. When they hit the paywall, customers can reset their cache, open an incognito browsing window, or just get news from other sites for the rest of the month.

Determine the smallest "taste" that provides the credibility and understanding needed for a prospect to subscribe, and no more. You want your trials to convert well, but it's also important to continue to try new things, even if you risk lower conversions. Nothing ventured, nothing gained!

Freemium ROI

A free trial is like a taste of filet mignon, the best thing on the menu, so that prospects understand and believe your promises. In contrast, a freemium subscription is like an all-you-can-eat hamburger bar—filling, not fancy. You can justify an investment in freemium in three ways:

1. Forming new habits: Use a freemium offer to demonstrate to prospects that they would use and value a membership or subscription.
2. Adding users to add value: Use a freemium offer to increase your overall numbers if your service benefits from the network effect.
3. As a marketing tactic: Use a freemium service to create avid fans who refer the service to other paying members. For example, you have a freemium subscription to SurveyMonkey and send a survey to your friend who happens to be a professional researcher. If your friend subscribes after learning about Survey-Monkey from your free survey, you are the acquisition source, or "marketing channel."

Each of these models has a return on investment that can be measured. For example, many news organizations use freemium to demonstrate to prospects that they're actually reading more than they think they are. If freemium subscribers keep hitting the paywall after reading 10 articles, they're likely to convert to paid—people who convert to paid after hitting the paywall can demonstrate ROI. Many organizations

> It's probably easiest to measure the value of someone as a marketing channel by assessing the value of new business people bring in through their referrals or viral connections.

assign a value to each new (nonpaying) member of their network, based on the impact it has on acquisition or retention of existing members. It's probably easiest to measure the value of someone as a marketing channel by assessing the value of new business people bring in through their referrals or viral connections. Ensure the ROI justifies the cost of the freemium offer. Having a high number of freemium subscribers might seem impressive, but only if it fits into a bigger strategy.

Cohort Analysis (by Month, Year, or Source)

To really understand what's happening within the organization, you need to tease the data apart by cohort. A cohort is a subset of customers, usually bound together by the date they became a customer, or by the acquisition source.

Once these groups have been distinguished, you can compare behavior in a particular period (i.e., first month or fifth month) or onboarding behavior across cohorts.

Looking at data in this way allows you to compare apples to apples, rather than blending away the variations. It's very useful to be able to understand how all customers behave, for example, in their first month of the subscription, or even in the first days. Start to develop rules of thumb about expected lifetime value, or drivers and timing of expected churn based on engagement.

Customer Engagement (Recency, Frequency, Depth; Engagement Score)

In a transactional business, when you sell someone a product, whether it's a shirt, a car, or an enterprise software solution, it's theirs. It doesn't matter whether they use the product every day, or not at all. Often, you realize the full customer lifetime value on the date of the initial transaction—when the car rolls out of the dealership or the software is installed.

With a forever transaction, the customer lifetime value (CLV) depends on how long the person chooses to continue subscribing. People can cancel at any time. Underutilization can be a big driver of churn, whether the customers aren't using the subscription because they haven't gotten around to it or because the service isn't useful to them.

It's your responsibility to make sure that your customers are using the service. You can track engagement in a number of different ways, including:

- Recency of engagement (when was the last time they used the subscription)
- Frequency of engagement (how often do they use the subscription)
- Depth/breadth of engagement (how many of the features do they use, and for how long)

Sometimes you can track the last engagement before an important event, like a cancellation or upgrade. These insights can be particularly valuable. An engagement score takes into account many of these metrics and ranks all customers by engagement. Then you can take actions contingent on the score. These actions might include an email, a phone call, or a special offer. The idea is to drive the behavior that results in engagement, which results in retention.

Table 13.2 summarizes these key metrics and their uses.

TABLE 13.2 Key Metrics and Their Uses

Metric	What It Is (How to Calculate)	Questions It Can Answer	Why It Matters
Customer Acquisition Cost (CAC)	How much you spend to attract a new customer—marketing/ad cost plus any direct trial expenses	How much did I spend to get this customer?	It doesn't matter if customers are cheap to get if they don't generate revenue. Conversely, you might spend a lot to attract a big spender.
Customer Lifetime Value (CLV)	The revenue customers brings in (directly and sometimes indirectly) between the time you acquire them and the time they cancel their subscription	What is my customer worth?	Not all customers are equal—customers who stay longer, join a higher-priced tier, or lead to additional new customers should be valued more highly (and justify higher CAC).
Expected CLV	Based on past customer *behavior*, by cohort, what would you predict to be the future value of a subscriber? Often calculated as ARPU / Churn Rate.	What will my revenue look like in the future?	Once you have analyzed cohorts' behavior and retention, you might be able to more accurately anticipate future cash flows.

(continued)

TABLE 13.2 Key Metrics and Their Uses, *continued*

Metric	What It Is (How to Calculate)	Questions It Can Answer	Why It Matters
CLV/CAC Ratio	CLV / CAC	Am I well positioned for sustainable growth?	It's OK to have (very) high CAC if it attracts customers with great CLV. But some investors will worry that the CAC is higher than they've seen in other businesses—which is a totally irrelevant point!
NPS Score	"On a scale of 0–10, how likely is it that you would recommend this to your friends, family, or business associates?" Customers that give you a 6 or below are Detractors, those with a score of 7 or 8 are called Passives, and those with a 9 or 10 are Promoters. NPS is % Promoters less % Detractors.	Are my customers happy enough to recommend my business? And if not, why not?	If they are making referrals, your acquisition costs are low and retention is likely to be high. Additionally, if they are not willing, they may be unhappy but not quite ready to cancel—it can be an early warning sign of low engagement and the potential to churn.

(continued)

TABLE 13.2 Key Metrics and Their Uses, *continued*

Metric	What It Is (How to Calculate)	Questions It Can Answer	Why It Matters
Churn	Number of subscribers (or revenue) that cancel in a period / subscribers (or revenue) at the start of the period	When and where are subscribers cancelling?	You can impact revenue and profitability much more easily by managing churn than by acquisition, and if you don't, you risk having a funnel that looks like a sieve.
Average Revenue per User (ARPU) or Account (ARPA)	Total monthly recurring revenue / total users (or accounts)	What is the average spend of my subscribers each period?	This can be a useful tool for determining changes in behavior among cohorts.
Annual Recurring Revenue (ARR)/ Monthly Recurring Revenue (MRR)	The total amount of revenue coming in each period (month or year) divided by the number of active customers, new and existing	What is the revenue stream for my business, month by month? How do I value the company?	These metrics take the average of your various pricing plans and billing periods into a single, consistent number so you can track trends over time. This metric is often the basis for company valuation.
Trial Conversion Rate	The number of people who take an offer divided by the total number of people offered it	Which offers are most attractive to my best customers?	Sometimes the most expensive offers are the best, but in many cases, companies give away more than they need to when offering a "taste" of their value.

(continued)

TABLE 13.2 Key Metrics and Their Uses, *continued*

Metric	What It Is (How to Calculate)	Questions It Can Answer	Why It Matters
Freemium Return on Investment	Direct revenue driven through freemium + indirect revenue (lead generation driven through freemium) divided by cost of freemium services	What does our organization get in return for offering something "for free, forever" to customers?	Many organizations do not think through the rationale for giving a freemium offer—organizations often think that a freemium option is required or expected.
Cohort Analysis (by month or year or by source)	Comparison of metrics such as churn and CAC by first month of subscription or by acquisition channel	What is the typical customer journey? What distinguishes our best customers? Why is a particular cohort not behaving as expected?	If you don't separate out cohorts, then any metric is averaged out and becomes less useful—for example, churn will seem artificially high in the month after a big acquisition campaign because more people cancel in the first period.
Customer Engagement	Depends on the business, but metrics that track recency, frequency, depth, and breadth of usage of subscription features	How are our customers using (or not using) the services they are paying for? Which behaviors do we see just before someone cancels or upgrades?	If customers aren't getting value for what they're paying for, they're more likely to churn. Also, engagement scores can identify best customers and lead to new feature development.

Common Challenges and Mistakes in Using Subscription Metrics

Even companies that track these metrics and use them to make business decisions sometimes face challenges or make mistakes. Here are a few of the most prevalent:

Focusing on Only a Few Metrics

Don't focus too heavily on too few metrics. A subscription dashboard should include metrics around acquisition, engagement, and retention. But many businesses overemphasize one over the others. New businesses tend to focus on adding customers. Business-to-business (B2B) SaaS companies get excited about those logos on their customer pages, and consumer-oriented organizations brag about new subscribers. But if those subscribers don't engage, and cancel before there's a positive customer lifetime value, acquisitions could actually signal debt accumulation. Many startups have burned through venture money to acquire customers that churn out almost as quickly as they sign up.

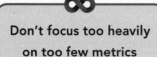
Don't focus too heavily on too few metrics

Many companies with a freemium model focus on engagement alone. They point out that (free) subscribers love their content but have no way of demonstrating any ROI on those freemium subscribers. Longtime subscription or membership businesses such as professional associations and newspapers often brag about member loyalty but have a hard time being relevant to today's prospects, those who are critical to tomorrow's business health. I pointed out earlier that once people have subscribed for a few periods, the likelihood of them canceling goes way down, so it makes sense that longtime subscribers are loyal. But when an organization isn't attracting new subscribers, it usually means that its offering hasn't evolved quickly and aggressively enough to be compelling to someone who is still actively considering options. When evaluating your own business health, use all three types of metrics: acquisition, engagement, and retention.

Using Someone Else's Benchmarks When Your Business Model Is Different

People ask me all the time for "typical" benchmarks to use with these metrics. It's impossible to answer a question like "What is an appropriate cost of acquisition (CAC)?" or "Is my churn rate too high?" without understanding the business model. If your subscription is for access to a fleet of Porsches and you're charging $2,000 a month, you can justify a much higher CAC than someone in the news business. If you offer a dating service and the average person takes three months to find true love, it's unlikely that your average subscriber will stay too long. Compare that to a music subscription where people might stay for years. You're much better off first determining what metrics make your business profitable and then push to improve your own benchmarks.

When an organization isn't attracting new subscribers, it usually means that its offering hasn't evolved quickly and aggressively enough to be compelling to someone who is still actively considering options.

Not Educating Your Investors and Board About Your Metrics

Even businesses that use the same metrics might have different benchmarks. You want your investors to understand how you look at the metrics and how you value success. Often, I see investors who focus too much on a single metric, such as growth of total customer base, or revenue, without understanding the importance of considering churn in conjunction with those metrics. Don't shy away from educating your investors on how you look at your business indicators and why.

Not Understanding the Distinction Between Metrics and Benchmarks

It's not enough just to track metrics—you have to develop benchmarks and look at trends within your own business. If CAC is increasing while retention is declining, there's probably a change in market conditions that you need to understand. Conversely, the benchmarks a software-as-a-service company uses, with business customers and high switching costs, will look different than the benchmarks of a consumer entertainment subscription, even if they are using the same metrics.

Letting Short-Term Metrics Outweigh Long-Term Strategy (The "Growth Hacker" Mindset)

Digital marketers often hack away at their metrics by making many micro-changes to their acquisition tactics and user-experience features. For example, they might experiment with a dozen different phrases, layouts, or discounts to see if they can move the needle. Often these changes are so frequent and so small they don't require a bigger understanding of subscriber, prospect, or even the longer-term strategy.

When you focus too intently on optimizing key metrics, you may lose sight of strategy. One SaaS company rewarded its marketing team for page views, so the team actually added unnecessary steps to their processes to grow the page view number. This created a worse experience for subscribers and over time resulted in lost revenue. The short-term goal eroded long-term customer satisfaction.

Subscription businesses only thrive when customers don't cancel; having a long-term focus is crucial. The key is to ensure that optimization occurs within larger business constraints and that the whole team understands the long-term drivers of success.

Freemium Issues

Many companies have had tremendous success with freemium models. Hotmail popularized the concept of viral growth with its free email service. LinkedIn gives away lots of value to members, attracting recruiters, salespeople, and jobseekers who are willing to pay for access to the information from the free members. Most news organizations give away some portion of their content on an ongoing basis, in addition to the deeper access provided to paying subscribers.

As a result, it can be tempting to incorporate freemium without justifying the investment. Only give away news content, for example, if you can prove that those consuming the free content eventually pay to subscribe, create value for paying subscribers, or attract paying subscribers. If they don't, there's no reason to give content away, unless you're doing it for altruistic or charitable reasons. For example, the *New York Times* opens up its paywall when hurricanes or major winter storms are bearing down on the mid-Atlantic coast. That's a case of using free to promote longer-term relationships.

The important thing is to track the return on investment you're getting on your freemium services. LinkedIn has been able to quantify the value of each new profile, understanding that the more professionals in its community, the more valuable the paid subscriptions become. And news organizations give away free articles because they know eventually some percentage of the freemium subscribers will upgrade. Tracking things like conversion and network effect, and coming up with metrics to quantify the value given away is the only way to justify a freemium model.

Metrics are powerful and important, and they can help you drive predictable, profitable revenue if you use them properly. Having analysts who are all over the metrics is critical, so that they can both track trends over time *and* continue to develop them and create new ones from the data you're gathering.

What to Do Next

- Identify the metrics that you want your investors and stakeholders to focus on.
- Determine how to educate them about those metrics; possibly schedule a meeting for this purpose.
- Additionally, identify leading indicator metrics that you want to use internally, for each process and each functional area, to provide early signs of improvements or weakness.

PART THREE Lead

Once you've established and scaled a successful recurring revenue business, the top priority is continued evolution. This is a cultural challenge. Change needs to be constant, but thoughtful enough to keep existing customers happy while attracting new ones.

With significant resources invested in scaling the business to this point, you might have other challenges demanding attention—infrastructure, financial investments, or business lines that have been neglected. You might be tempted to harvest extra revenue from existing customers to hit an important financial goal. Unexpected disruptions may prompt you to rethink your entire strategy.

This part will guide you as you maintain the leadership role you've worked hard to establish, and maximize ongoing relationships with your customers, subscribers, or members.

Chapter 14: Forever Is a Long Time: Don't Take Shortcuts

Chapter 15: Continue to Iterate

Chapter 16: Stay Forever Young: Avoid Aging with Your Members

Chapter 17: Protect Your Members from Subscription Fatigue

Chapter 18: Going Global with the Forever Transaction

Chapter 19: Emerging Trends—Forever Is Here Now

14 Forever Is a Long Time: Don't Take Shortcuts

In February of 2019, David Heinemeier Hansson, cofounder of Ruby on Rails, launched a Tweet storm about his experience trying to cancel his subscription to SiriusXM with this expletive-ridden diatribe: "Oh f*ck off @SIRIUSXM. I don't want to 'discuss my options,' I just want to cancel your sh*t without the hassle of having to call your f*cking hotline. F*ck."[1] The tweet hit a nerve, prompting dozens of retweets and over 1,000 likes. So many of us have had this experience of not being able to find the cancel button and end the relationship.

SiriusXM isn't the only company that has drawn the ire of subscribers who feel unfairly treated by subscription businesses. In 2015, Kate Hudson's Fabletics faced a storm of negative press.[2] More than 1,200 consumers complained to the Better Business Bureau. Many of them had taken advantage of the company's "new VIP member exclusive" offer of an active wear outfit for just $25 without seeing the fine print authorizing the company to bill them for a recurring revenue program at up to $45 a month. Fabletics required cancelation by phone—no digital option was available, making consumers even more angry.

FIGURE 14.1 David Heinemeier Hansson's Infamous Rant

It can be tempting to use the structure of a subscription business to shortcut your way to revenue goals. Many organizations are under tremendous pressure to hit quarterly goals, and many executives are compensated on short-term objectives. Maybe you're thinking about your *next* role and want your financial results to look good for the next employer. But building your organization on a true "forever promise" means making every decision as if you'll never sell the business. Focus on the long term, and avoid strategies that directly conflict with forever. Pay attention to the following symptoms of short-termism in your own business.

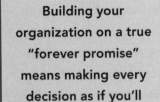

Building your organization on a true "forever promise" means making every decision as if you'll never sell the business.

The "Growth at All Costs" Problem

Subscription models are having a moment. According to McKinsey & Company's 2018 white paper "Thinking Inside the Subscription Box,"[3] the subscription e-commerce market alone has grown by more than 100 percent a year for the five years from 2012 to 2017. Zuora's Q4 2018 Subscription Index report claims subscription companies have grown more than 300 percent in the past seven years, pointing out "an average company in the Subscription Economy has grown its revenue by 321% since the launch of the index in January 2012, a compound annual growth rate of 18.1%."[4] The report further claims that overall, subscription businesses are growing revenues about five times more quickly than S&P 500 company revenues and US retail sales.

Companies using membership and subscription as key components of their business models, like Netflix, Amazon, Microsoft, and LinkedIn, are among the most valuable companies in the world. And, in Spring, 2019, Apple announced a major investment in subscription services, to shift the balance away from a total reliance on premium hardware, the growth of which had been slowing.[5]

To justify higher valuations—which are often based on revenue multiples—and to attract investors, many companies focus disproportionately on new customer acquisition and topline revenue growth. They tend to ignore other metrics important to assessing business model health, most notably lifetime customer value. A fast-growing profession called *growth hacking* focuses on attracting customers by continually tinkering with marketing activities throughout the sales funnel, with a goal of driving incremental improvements in customer growth. They use email, copywriting, channel experiments, analytics, and search engine optimization (SEO) among other tactics, all with a goal of amping up acquisition. Growth hackers iterate rapidly and look for lower-cost channels. I'm generally a fan of the discipline. In fact, some of the practice's thought leaders claim that rapid prototyping is a part of growth hacking, and that any "good" growth hacker only tests sustainable, profitable tactics.

However, as the name suggests, this approach usually happens in a vacuum, where growth is completely separated from engagement and retention numbers. The value created for the subscriber is often overlooked. Some growth hackers try things without enough concern for how their tactics fit with a larger strategy. As a result, you risk running acquisition campaigns that might mislead customers about their offer or that attract a particular type of customer who is quick to sign up *and* quick to cancel.

Organizations with a strong growth hacker culture often lose money on every new customer. That's okay if the organization has deep pockets and a long-term plan to generate revenue from a community of subscribers operating at a loss, or if they've built a clear customer lifetime value (CLV) model demonstrating a path to profitability, market-share dominance, or successful exit (depending on their overall strategy). However, growth hackers don't necessarily have revenue generation responsibilities; their objectives may conflict with long-term revenue.

MoviePass implemented a growth strategy in 2018 when it offered its subscribers virtually unlimited movies at nearly any theater for just $9.99 a month. MoviePass took this approach for several reasons. First, the parent company's larger plan was to collect data. It never planned to make money on the MoviePass revenue; it had a bigger strategy that assessed a value for each new member. Second, the company was attempting a "land grab" to change how consumers consumed movies in theaters. MoviePass couldn't sustain the bargain-basement pricing and, after changing the offer in 2019 to $14.95 for a limited selection of movies and theaters, lost 90 percent of its subscribers within a year.[6]

> Organizations with a strong growth hacker culture often lose money on every new customer.

The "Extract Every Drop of Value" Problem

When I was in business school, there were two kinds of parking permits—A and C. Cs had limited spaces, while As could park in A lots and

C lots. The problem was, there weren't enough spots. The university's solution? Change the C lots to A lots. Still not enough spots, but now everyone paid more because you had to have an A pass to park within a mile of the classroom. This felt very unfair to students because the scarcity problem was manufactured by the university in the first place.

Organizations talk a lot about customers' willingness to pay and want to extract as much value from customers as possible. I understand this sentiment. If you have the only water in the desert, or the antidote for a painful ailment, it can be tempting to charge a huge premium. But there's a risk here, especially for businesses that depend on long-term relationships with customers—it's just a matter of time before a competitor enters with a less expensive, "disruptive" alternative. When that happens, your customers will not only switch—they'll realize that you were gouging them and won't trust you. By focusing on the long-term relationship, you can do much to "disruption proof" your business.

In 2019, SoulCycle, the spinning studio company, realized that its members cared so much about getting their favorite bikes and classes that they made sure to log in Mondays at 12 when the week's classes became available. As a result, SoulCycle introduced "SoulEarly," which allows members to sign up on Sunday for a 50 percent premium on standard rates.[7] Members can also "earn" SoulEarly credits by buying more classes. On the one hand, this seems like a great example of adding a new value tier. On the other hand, this is a case of charging more for limited inventory and creating status for spend. There's a risk here that this short-term revenue generator might have a long-term result of turning off members who don't want to be second-class citizens. And Peloton's all too happy to take on the SoulCycle refugees as members—at a fraction of the cost.

The Cash Cow Problem (or Don't Harvest Too Early)

Every once in a while, prospects call me for help "cash cowing" their business. I'm referring to Boston Consulting Group's famous growth-share matrix created by Bruce D. Henderson (Figure 14.2). Cash cows are low-growth businesses that nevertheless generate profitable revenue. Usually organizations harvest such businesses and use the proceeds to invest in future opportunities. Harvesting (pulling in revenue without investing in the long-term health and growth of the business) is fine if you *know* you're going to be leaving that market.

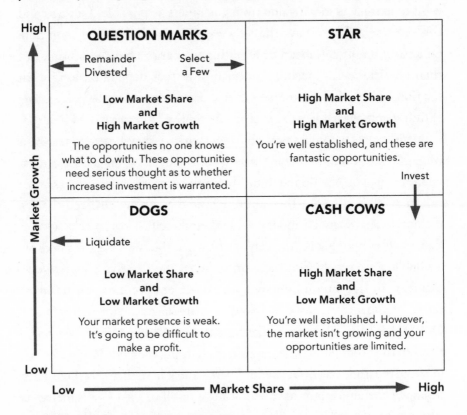

FIGURE 14.2 Growth-Share Matrix

Source: Martin Reeves, Sandy Moose , and Thijs Venema, "BCG Classics Revisited: The Growth-Share Matrix," BCG, June 4, 2014, https://www.bcg.com/en-us/publications/2014/growth-share-matrix-bcg -classics-revisited.aspx. Accessed March 25, 2019.

Too often, organizations take a harvesting mindset in businesses while still acting as if the business is going to produce revenue like a high-growth, high-market-share star. This often happens when the organization has become distracted by short-term goals. In a rush to hit those goals, they make decisions that might kill the golden goose (mixing metaphors, I know!). For example, a newspaper whose subscription base is shrinking might raise fees, with little notice among loyal subscribers, to hit revenue targets.

Continuity programs have long been guilty of this mindset. Remember 13 CDs for a penny? That was music continuity. Today's continuity programs include Proactiv for acne, Fabletics for athletic clothing, and the dozens of something-of-the-month clubs. My current favorite is Cowgirl Creamery's Cheese-of-the-Month Club. Subscribers pay in advance each period for physical product delivery. Some services focus on replenishment, others on discovery or variety, and some both. Although there are some highly ethical and transparent continuity programs (including Proactiv and Fabletics), many of these types of businesses are notorious for thwarting cancellation and hiding fees that drive costs higher than originally advertised. These decisions and tactics (all of which really happen) might generate a little more revenue now, but they will frustrate subscribers, resulting in fewer sign-ups and more cancellations.

The Miami Heat Invests in Forever with Fickle Fans: A Case Study

Kim Stone, a veteran executive and vice president of service at the professional basketball team the Miami Heat, focused on fan experience, and particularly the experience of loyal fans and season ticket holders, as a means of building loyalty in a fickle market during her 15-plus-year tenure in the role.[8] Miami has a crowded sports landscape, with professional hockey, football, and baseball, as well as basketball and high-level college athletic teams. It's also a popular destination for outdoor recreation and nightlife. But service is a tricky differentiator, and it doesn't work well as an acquisition tool. The value of service is only recognized after it has been experienced. Its true role is in retention. Most organization claim they provide (or want to provide) good service, but it takes a long-term commitment. The payoff takes a while to realize, and it's easy to cut back as a shortcut to quick cost savings.

The Heat consciously pursues a strategy of high-level and meaningful customer service to secure the loyalty of fans through down seasons as well as winning ones. Season ticket holders are "Season Ticket Members" to the Heat, emphasizing the connection the team wants to make with the people they serve and the sense of belonging and status they want fans to feel.

The team embraced this emphasis on experience when Shaquille O'Neal left the team during the 2007/2008 season after three and a half years with the Heat. O'Neal had megastar powers of attraction, and following his trade to the Phoenix Suns, season ticket sales in Miami plummeted. Understanding the importance of long-term member retention, Heat president Pat Riley separated sales and service into two departments with different metrics. This organization structure was used for more than 10 years and has served to instill a philosophy of fan-centricity that continues to this day.

Service reps prioritize building a personal relationship with each season ticket member, acting almost as concierges. They are empowered to do "whatever it takes" within reason to delight their members—a Dwyane Wade jersey for a kid's birthday or flowers for a season ticket member's anniversary when special occasions are celebrated at the arena. Members enjoy events with players, get better pricing on tickets, and have reserved access at the most conveniently located ticket gate. They enjoy a sliding scale of preferred pricing at concession stands, topping out at 30 percent for those who have been members for 10 years or more. Members also get priority selection for in-game entertainment, like the half-court shooting competition. When a season ticket member is announced as a contestant, it's as "Robbie Baxter, our season ticket member since 2001."

Stone says, "We want season ticket members to bask in the glory of being a season ticket member in front of their friends." She also notes that technology such as a mobile app and season ticket member web portal provide convenience and utility for members to support the relationship. But the relationship itself is at the core.

When things are going well for the team, with a winning record and marquee players, it can be tempting to raise prices for everyone. But the

Heat has resisted this temptation. In 2010 the Heat got the big three: LeBron James, Dwyane Wade, and Chris Bosh. They doubled down on season ticket holders. They invested in services to ensure that when the big-name players left, as they inevitably would, the relationship with fans transitioned from the back of the jersey to the front.

In 2019, Stone left Miami to become general manager of the Chase Center, the new San Francisco arena home to the Golden State Warriors of the NBA. The Warriors have dominated the NBA with several All-Star players and three championships in five years. The burning question is, however, as players like Kevin Durant move on, and the record sinks, will the fans stay loyal? Will the Warriors pursue a customer-centric strategy that can survive losing seasons and lost marquee players?

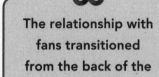

The relationship with fans transitioned from the back of the jersey to the front.

The Warriors have been locking fans into long-term "contracts" at their fabulous new stadium, charging $35,000 for the privilege of buying season tickets (tickets themselves are hundreds of dollars each), and requiring members to buy the full season or forfeit membership.[9] When the team was winning, fans didn't seem to mind, but I wonder how they'll feel when the team isn't as exciting. The Warriors have set the bar high for joining; hopefully their new stadium will provide the service and experience to justify the commitment. No shortcuts.

Root Causes

Why do businesses make short-term decisions that cause long-term relationship damage? There are many reasons. Some organizations fear that the subscription value itself won't drive engagement, loyalty, and profitability. Some want to maximize the value of members who trust the organization so much that they neglect to read the fine print. There are two schools of thought here—some believe in "buyer beware," while others (myself included) believe that trust must be earned. Many financially oriented owners and executives don't understand the mechanics (and requirements) of successful subscription business and don't realize that short-term harvesting can do long-term damage. Finally, executives and investors focused on their own exit strategies may do whatever it takes to generate attractive metrics in advance of that exit.

> Don't choose clever over forever.

Sometimes companies get distracted by short-term goals. Occasionally, the short term is the only priority, and the company must hit certain arbitrary milestones in order to keep the doors open or win financing. But unfortunately, a short-term emphasis destroys the brand value you've spent so much time and effort to build. Remember, the beauty of a forever transaction is the annuity-like nature of the revenue stream. A business that focuses on the long-term well-being of customers earns the right to autopay. Don't choose clever over forever.

What to Do Next

- If you haven't already, establish a guiding principle to keep the team focused on customer success. If you have one, make sure everyone knows about it.
- Consider putting someone on your support or success team into a more prominent role; ensure this person is a regular speaker at all-hands meetings.
- Find a way to have the customer "in the room" at key moments, and institutionalize ways to keep the customer front-of-mind in structured and unstructured meetings.

15 Continue to Iterate

When I worked as a product manager at an enterprise software company in the mid-1990s, our work revolved around the Golden Compact Disk (CD). Every 18 months or so, we'd release a new version of our product. Engineers dedicated months to building the product, working at a fevered pitch as the release date approached. When the release date arrived, they'd burn a master CD with the entire fixed code for the new product. That master was a CD with a gold outer coating instead of the usual aluminum or silver coating, to make it stand out from other CDs (back in the day, tech offices were filled with CDs). We'd produce and distribute copies of this updated version of our software to all of our customers with a big "ta da". Inevitably, there were features customers loved and those they hated, as well as some bugs—features that didn't quite work as promised. We'd send patches to fix the bugs and promise that the unloved features would be fixed in the next release—18 months out.

Things have changed in Silicon Valley. Companies like Netflix, Oracle, and Google change their code on a daily, if not hourly, basis. Changes reach customers immediately through the model known as software-as-a-service (SaaS). The customers (subscribers) no longer own the software, they only access it. Because subscribers can cancel access to the software, software makers have a greater motivation to improve it. In some cases, their enhancements merit a price increase, either as a new level of subscription or as an add-on. Sometimes they lower the pricing due to changes in the market.

> Because you've made a forever promise, you need to ensure that products and pricing continue to support the value you're creating for the people you serve.

Whether you're offering physical products, digital content, professional services, or access to a community, over time your products will change. You might add features, but you are also likely to remove features. There are good reasons to raise *and lower* prices over time. Because you've made a forever promise, you need to ensure that products and pricing continue to support the value you're creating for the people you serve. This chapter provides some tips to do that.

Fine-Tune Delivery to Keep Your Forever Promise Relevant

While you want your promise to be clear, specific, and honest, it also has to be meaty enough to be interesting. What happens when the forever promise becomes uninteresting or too small? When Netflix launched, its forever promise of "broad selection of professionally created video content delivered with cost certainty in the most efficient way possible" was new and compelling. Other companies then went direct to consumers with similar promises—HBO, Hulu, Amazon Prime, and even CBS. Comcast started offering a wide range of movies and shows on demand. At this point, Netflix had to add unique content to its promise. Breadth, cost-certainty, and convenience were no longer enough.

The same challenges apply to long-established institutions. It's interesting to watch parking garages evolve, as their promise of "helping travelers come and go efficiently" has been outdone by ridesharing services like Lyft and Uber. A 2016 article by the Local Government Commission notes that "autonomous vehicles could erase the need for up to 90% of our current parking lots in the next 15 years."[1] What *could* parking lots offer consumers to make travel more efficient? Maybe the extra space could provide safe access to ride shares, like many airport parking garages are doing. Or garages could aggregate additional services for the smaller group of cars still parking—making parking lots a place to drop off and pick up dry-cleaning and meals, or even have gas delivery and car washes. But any parking lot company that thinks the same volume of drivers will be parking there in the next few years is missing the opportunity to continue evolving for the customers they know best.

From Weight Loss to Wellness— Weight Watchers Rebrands as WW

In *The Membership Economy*, I held up Weight Watchers as "one of the best examples of a successful membership that has continually evolved to meet its members' needs."[2] I still think it's true, but it's worth looking at what's happened in the space and some of the strategic decisions the current CEO, Mindy Grossman, has made.

The challenge any weight-loss company faces is that once people have either successfully lost the weight or given up on weight loss for the time being, they cancel the membership. As a result, the more successful the product, the less time a member spends on the program. Additionally, as weight loss inherently has an end when users reach their goals, the average member stops using the program after six to nine months. It is very hard to track membership in terms of years rather than months.

One of the smartest things Weight Watchers has built into its model is the concept of a "lifetime member." Weight Watchers members pay every week until they reach and maintain their self-defined goal weight (which must be at least a loss of 10 percent of body weight at sign-up) for six weeks. After that, participating in Weight Watchers is free forever, as long as members stay within three pounds of their goal weight and attend meetings at least once a month. If they exceed weight or miss a month, they have to pay for meetings until they're back in compliance.

This approach has effectively achieved several important objectives. Most important, lifetime membership provides a system for helping members maintain their goal weight—their forever promise. It also means that success stories attend meetings—maybe for the rest of their lives—serving as role models and ambassadors to new members. Should a lifetime member fall off the wagon, there's the possibility of additional direct revenue for Weight Watchers.

However, it appears that this model is no longer effective enough for the company. Weight Watchers has publicly talked about the struggle to attract members beyond its current demographic, primarily moms from the middle of the country. The company faces competition from all sides. There are weight-loss apps both free and paid, like Noom, Aaptiv, and even MyFitnessPal. There's a proliferation of new diets, with associated coaching, food, and supplements—including Whole30, keto, paleo, and the Longevity diet. Perhaps the biggest threat comes from the many companies trying to claim leadership in the wellness space. Gwyneth Paltrow's Goop garners a lot of attention. Fitbit, Apple Watch, and other wearables companies are introducing weight loss as one tenet of a full range of healthy behaviors, alongside exercise, meditation, and better sleep hygiene.

So Grossman is redefining the forever promise, a bold and risky move. Instead of promising weight loss and a lifetime at a healthy weight, she's promising the broader, more inclusive but also more nebulous "wellness." Her goal is to transform Weight Watchers into a "wellness company," as the desire to be well never ends. She changed the name of the company to WW, standing for Wellness that Works. The company also brought on spokespeople whose desire was to live healthier rather than lose weight.

Will it work? The jury is still out. It may be a larger market, but people may not feel the same urgency to be "well" as they do to stop feeling overweight. It may be a challenge to keep the loyal Weight Watchers market with a new message that no longer targets the core audience.

Use Product-Market Fit (PMF) as a Key to Continuous Improvement

Companies generate and store oceans of customer data, but often it sits unused, or is presented without context and not applied to actual decision making. However, organizations are increasingly applying principles of data science to analyze data.

Some investors are pushing for better analysis and consistent reporting of the insights in customer data. One such investor is Jonathan Hsu, cofounder and general partner of Tribe Capital, who earned a doctorate in physics and helped to form and lead the data science and analytics organization at Facebook before making the transition to venture capital.[3]

Hsu spends a lot of time thinking about how data science can be applied specifically to assessing product-market fit (PMF). PMF is important because it's the smallest unit of value exchange between an organization and its customers. It happens when the market wants and needs the product the company is offering. The term was coined by Andy Rachleff, cofounder of Benchmark Capital, and incorporates ideas developed by Don Valentine, founder of Sequoia, a leading venture capital firm.[4]

Rachleff explained it like this: "If you address a market that really wants your product—if the dogs are eating the dog food—then you can screw up almost everything in the company and you will succeed. Conversely, if you're really good at execution but the dogs don't want to eat the dog food, you have no chance of winning."[5]

> "If you address a market that really wants your product—if the dogs are eating the dog food—then you can screw up almost everything in the company and you will succeed. Conversely, if you're really good at execution but the dogs don't want to eat the dog food, you have no chance of winning."
>
> —Andy Rachleff, Cofounder, Benchmark Capital

Most companies have a lot of usage data, which can be useful for assessing PMF. Hsu sees PMF reporting as a new kind of accounting. In accounting, you take a pile of data (a ledger) and turn it into something useful (an income statement or balance sheet). In a PMF report, you take a big quantity of usage data and turn it into valuable insights about the market needs. To assess PMF, Hsu suggests three types of analysis, each narrow enough to be more useful than a "pile of data" but broad enough to be applicable to many types of organizations and businesses.[6] Together they create a kind of accounting statement for PMF:

1. **Growth accounting.** Assess your growth rate. In addition to new revenue, track expansion revenue (same customers, new spend) and contraction revenue (same customer, declining spend). You might also track whether the new spend is on new products or more of the same products. With any kind of subscription, there's a difference between acquiring a new dollar from a new customer and an additional dollar from an existing customer. You need to understand whether dollars lost were due to a decrease in spending or a customer leaving (churn). Businesses with subscriptions often have the healthiest growth because the recurring revenue is so profitable.

2. **Cohorts.** Track your customers from acquisition through departure—the entire relationship. This analysis includes customer lifetime value (CLV), cohort customer retention, and cohort revenue retention. Analyzing the customers' journey as well as their CLV based on shared customer traits, like lead source or timing of initial transaction, gives you a granular understanding of where the value is coming from, one cohort at a time. This approach is better than averaging, which is dangerous because earlier customers behave differently than customers acquired later. Additionally, a cohort of 100 customers might behave differently. Some might stay a few months, while others cancel right away. Or, if you don't have a subscription, some might spend $100 each month, while others only spend $5. You need to track retention of customers, but you also need to track retention of *dollars*—ensuring that you're optimizing not only

for acquiring new customers but also for retaining the best and most valuable customers for the long term.

3. **PMF distribution.** You need to continually evaluate the distribution of usage data. I have spoken before about tracking recency, frequency, and breadth/depth of usage. But it's not enough to take averages. For example, knowing "average minutes spent" isn't as useful as understanding the median and top quintile. Once you average everything together, you don't see how big the spread is and whether there are clusters—for example, if the top 10 percent of customers spend $100 and the bottom 90 percent spend

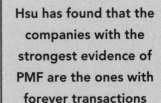

Hsu has found that the companies with the strongest evidence of PMF are the ones with forever transactions

$10 each, the average is $19. You miss the whole story—that a few customers are very valuable but the rest aren't. Similarly, for a software-as-a-service (SaaS) business, knowing average customer value (ACV) is useful (the analog of the "average" level of PMF), but knowing the median and various percentiles is usually more useful. You'll find some customers use your product regularly for a narrow, specific use case, others use many features but only occasionally, and some never use the product after the initial purchase. Some of these customers are finding more value than others, and usage often correlates with perceived value. PMF distribution is about building a granular understanding of who is actually engaging with your product and how.

Hsu has tested these three approaches with thousands of products and companies, including large organizations with multiple products, each of which may have different levels of PMF. Hsu has found that the companies with the strongest evidence of PMF are the ones with forever transactions, whether they're subscription-based like Slack or Netflix, or are simply highly predictable recurring revenue businesses like Amazon or Uber. Specifically, in the context of early stage companies, the detailed picture of recurring or recurring-like behavior tends to persist as the company scales. By contrast, when the product behavior is nowhere near recurring, it's much less clear how customers will unfold as they age. An example of a nonrecurring business is the jewelry, gifts, and accessories retailer Tiffany, where the purchases are few and not predictable. After all, how many engagement rings does one person need?

Product portfolio analysis is key. Some cohorts are going to mature with the product, but new cohorts, particularly those with different demographics (usually younger) might want a different product that makes good on the same forever promise. Additionally, you might want to keep adding features for your most engaged and/or longstanding subscribers. If I'm a marathon runner, I might need basic support to get started, but once I break the four-hour mark, I might need a different training plan and nutritional coaching. Older, longstanding readers might prefer print, people choosing their news source now might prefer digital or mobile video content.

Avoid Feature Bloat

Most product teams are very familiar with the idea of starting with a minimum viable product (MVP)—the smallest, leanest product that solves the customer's problem. Organizations layer in additional features and benefits to more deeply support their customers' needs. But if you've been successful for an extended period of time and added lots of features, it may be time to start retiring products and features. It can be tempting to leave all features in the subscription, but there's a cost to maintaining each feature. Too many features can confuse customers, and they might not be able to find the ones they value amidst all the older ones. As anyone who's ever cleaned out a closet knows, you can find and enjoy what you want much more readily if you get rid of what you really don't need anymore. The hard part is that there's always that one loyal customer who loves that obsolete feature or product—and is really vocal. Even if you know that the right thing to do is to change anyway, and maybe let that individual know, privately, why you are making the change, it can be uncomfortable to do. So you may end up providing faxing services, or VHS formats, even though it takes up resources and mindshare you could otherwise use to invest in tomorrow's members. So, even though it's tough to disappoint a loyal customer, you may find that keeping the feature they love costs your company too much.

Keep an Eye on the (Competitive) Horizon

It's important to remember the *market* part of product-market fit—not just which individual customers are engaging, but also the other options they have. This is a place where many companies stumble. Continued competitive landscape assessment is important. It's not only companies with similar products you need to beware of, but also those companies that are solving your customer's bigger problems.

Businesses with strong recurring revenue have solid PMF, but they're also much more predictable by cohort. Their growth in CLV comes from the ongoing engagement customer, which makes for recurring revenue, not just from the initial transaction. Focus on where the growth is happening, which cohorts are engaging with the products, and what those people need. By matching that information with the changes in the broader market, you'll have ample insights for your product road map.

> It's not only companies with similar products you need to beware of, but also those companies that are solving your customer's bigger problems.

Dawn Sweeney, CEO of the National Restaurant Association, told me about a game she plays with her team.[7] Imagine your most strategic employee left your organization, found a great digital technologist and an investor with deep pockets, and decided to go after your "forever promise" from scratch. With none of your organization's legacy baggage, what would that new team do?

Most banks promise to help customers make and receive payments in the easiest way possible. Along the way, they focused on some of their products, like credit cards. But if you were starting from scratch, you might want to start with the mobile phone, which is more convenient and provides more functionality than a plastic card. This kind of thought exercise works for nearly any business or industry. For example, speaking with the International Car Wash Association, I suggested that a car wash might offer a forever promise: "Your car will always be clean with minimal effort from you." If that's the promise, I don't want to come into the car wash at all. I'd prefer the car wash to come to me (to my car) and just make sure it was clean periodically.

How would car washes deliver this promise? Owners should spend less effort shaving minutes or seconds off the time it takes the car to go through the car wash—the current goal of most car wash innovation—and more effort figuring out how to go where the cars are with a mobile service. The car wash owners I spoke with didn't want to make that available because they'd already invested so much in their real estate and capital investments. I understand their concern—but they're unwittingly creating a disruptive opportunity for the many mobile car wash services, and for services like Filld, which fills your gas tank in your driveway in the dead of night. And now, they face a much bigger challenge, as autonomous vehicles promise to change the landscape of cars yet again.

Don't limit your evaluation to feature comparisons with your most direct competitors. And don't start with the product. Instead, always start with the customer's needs and challenge yourself to identify better ways to more fully meet those needs. Keep finding and resolving pain points. To keep your forever promise relevant, continuously evaluate how you could better deliver on it. Be willing to change products, processes, and even your team members. Consider your competition, but also consider other broader trends in how your target audience solves their problems. And continue to use PMF accounting so you can recognize changes in engagement. It's always best to start with the promise, though, and work backward from there.

What to Do Next

- Make sure you are able to track the right PMF data, and that you have processes to implement the insights you gain from your assessments. If you aren't able to track it yet, be resourceful—do interviews, send surveys, and use what you have.
- Listen carefully to your early cohorts as well as to the cohorts who surprise you by not taking your offer. Incorporate that learning into future iterations.
- Resist the temptation to put product and service improvements on the back burner. You are never "done," because your goal is delivering on your promise in the best way possible. Your goal is not "getting a product to market," it's helping to make your customer's life better.

16

Stay Forever Young: Avoid Aging with Your Members

Pål Nedregotten is the EVP of Amedia, Norway's largest publisher of local media titles.[1] For several years, Amedia has been revamping its approach to creating news worth paying for, using a subscriber-first strategy. The leaders learned a lot. They learned that what their editorial team produced most was read least. Local readers prioritize transportation, healthcare, and social, crime/police/legal, real estate, and accidents/incidents. They didn't read as much about culture (which comprised the highest number of stories), politics/public sector, or international sports coverage.

Readers loved hyperlocal live video feeds, even with basic recording quality. One of the most popular digital articles featured a live feed of the minister of fisheries visiting a local village to talk about fishing rights. And subscribers loved having access to third-tier Norwegian football (soccer), something the television stations didn't bother with. Amedia discovered that one reason younger audiences weren't subscribing (or reading) their titles had less to do with "millennials don't like news" and more to do with "millennials don't like how we're doing news." Most of the articles were about older people, dealt with topics older people found interesting, and featured photos of older people.

Amedia had been serving its existing subscribers so well that it was ignoring its future. As a result of this assessment and refocusing, the organization was able to attract a younger base of customers and identify new ways to generate revenue for formerly struggling local papers.

While Amedia recognized the problem and adapted, many organizations don't think it's an issue to have an aging cohort. From newspapers, to professional associations and nonprofits, to country clubs, many of the longest-standing subscription businesses are risking the trap of becoming irrelevant by focusing too much on longstanding members.

The Dark Side of Loyalty

Many organizations enjoying great success with a loyal cohort cater so much to their current members that they forget to stay relevant for *tomorrow's* members. Longtime members are often engaged and vocal. They may serve on an advisory board. In a nonprofit, they may have governance roles, so their voices are powerful. In many member-oriented organizations, the employees are also treated like members. While this is often a good thing, employees can age along with the customer cohort. As a result, the organization lacks a diversity of voices and continues to offer products, processes, and services aligned with the needs of the aging cohort.

> Many organizations enjoying great success with a loyal cohort cater so much to their current members that they forget to stay relevant for *tomorrow's* members.

When you see a customer-centric organization with aging members, it's often because the organization has stopped listening to tomorrow's members—both their prospects and their newest subscribers. The organization may have begun as a disruptor, appealing to edgy prospects looking for a better way. But with success, that organization may grow insular and immutable. It looks and behaves as it did 20, 30, or more years ago. And it exhibits its greatest loyalty to existing members, rather than the mission of those members in its entirety. As a result, the organization's offerings are no longer relevant to new prospective customers, who are still considering alternatives.

The Problem with Loyal Congregations

Pastors, rabbis, priests, and other religious leaders often struggle to attract and retain new members in the Membership Economy. For better or worse, prospective congregants sometimes behave like consumers, especially when making a decision about which organization to join. These modern seekers have access to better information about options; what once worked to attract members may not work anymore. Having a majority of elderly parishioners can be a signal that current offerings aren't "competitive" or relevant to parishioners in 2020. Members who joined a long time ago may not have "shopped for alternatives" since.

In many cases, religious organizations find that their services and approach were optimized at peak appeal when today's members first joined. Once organizations enjoy some measure of success, they often stop innovating, thus becoming less able to attract new members. If you have an older community, it's tempting to create services optimized for that current membership—after all, they're the ones you see every day, and they're the ones who speak up. It's "customer-centric" right? But beware of focusing only on today's (and not tomorrow's) members. If all of your programming options are held at midday and have words like "retirement" in the title, it's exponentially harder to reach working adults and families. How can you evolve and innovate your programming to serve the working mom? The millennial? The college student?

This problem can be exacerbated by a governance structure in which longtime members have the most power. Many churches, synagogues, and mosques are led by older people who have been members for many years. It's great to have the wisdom and long memories of such members, but organizations need to hear the voices of tomorrow's members too, or they risk not attracting them.

An aging cohort suggests that the organization has stopped reaching out to new prospective members (a marketing issue), or that the organization delivers on the problem in a way that is no longer optimal (a product issue). This point applies to more than just religious institutions. Any membership organization with a graying population, such as news organizations, professional associations, or popular entertainment franchises, can find itself a victim of its own success and longevity.

If you're a leader of a congregation struggling to attract new members, there are options. Target people who've already tried a digital-only religious community but didn't find it satisfying. There's an opportunity to win them back to a more intimate experience. For example, if your prospective parishioners are going online and realizing that there's no substitute for a live, human connection, you could try something like this: "If you want more than inspiring speeches over your EarPods, join us for live connections with your neighbors every week." Or: "Meditation is good, but meditation with a strong spiritual framework is better."

> ∞
>
> An aging cohort suggests that the organization has stopped reaching out to new prospective members (a marketing issue), or that the organization delivers on the problem in a way that is no longer optimal (a product issue).

Another option is to evolve the services your organization provides. If your prospective members use digital tools to research local houses of worship and don't choose you, or if prospects seem to prefer a digital-only solution, you might need to make major changes. The needs of prospective members evolve, and better ways of delivering value emerge too. Of course, this is true of businesses as well—members' needs are always evolving, as are the tools to provide and package benefits that meet those needs.

Don't Forget Tomorrow's Members

Remember, part of the beauty of a forever promise is that once customers are committed, they stop behaving like a buyer and start acting like a member, no longer evaluating other options. Even if existing customers say they're happy, it may be inertia talking. Meanwhile, the options available to uncommitted prospects continue to expand.

Prospects might be treated like outsiders when they do join, and therefore not feel welcomed. One professional association's entire governance board was comprised of people over 50 (white men, actually) concerned with issues of succession planning and retirement. New members of the profession were paying off student loans and seeking the right next job. Guess which topic was programmed for the annual meeting.

This is a challenging dilemma. "New members have different needs than long-term members who comprise governing boards," says Robert Skrob, an expert on association subscription memberships and the author of *Retention Point*.[2] "New members need tactical benefits to launch their careers, while long-timers want networking, advocacy and leadership opportunities." Remember how shocked the tennis establishment was by players who chose not to wear tennis whites, or dared to wear a catsuit? The problem with many memberships is that they are cliquey and resistant to change. Make sure your front door stays welcoming.

Refreshing Your Offering While Staying True to Your Mission—the HFMA Story

The Healthcare Financial Management Association (HFMA) is an instructive example of member-centricity, and of an organization willing to undergo a two-and-a-half-year journey to fully reinvent itself. With a focus on helping hospital CFOs "lead, learn, and connect" (the core pillars of the organization), the association generated 2018 revenues of nearly $26 million, has about 38,000 official members, and has been around for more than 70 years.[3]

Like many organizations that have enjoyed longstanding success, HFMA had developed a sizeable portfolio with dozens of products to support its core values—training courses, conferences, e-books, webinars, certifications, an online community, and so on. The organization's structure corresponded to its product and service lines—membership, education, publications, research, and other departments—not around its promise of helping members learn, lead, and connect. When Garth Jordan joined HFMA in May of 2016 as Chief Strategy Officer,[4] the organization was buckling under the sheer weight of its massive product lines and members were feeling nickel-and-dimed, a natural but negative outcome of product proliferation. Subsequently, Jordan conducted a rigorous and inclusive design thinking exercise, which required staff and the governing board directors to shadow or interview members. By August of 2017, Jordan had gathered enough qualitative member data to create key insights about the value HFMA members were really needing from the association. These four key insights informed everything they did going forward:

1. Offer *easy and open* access to relevant information.
2. *Collaborate* across boundaries to influence change around them.
3. *Navigate the pace and complexity of the change* around them, and to be "the smartest person in the room" about the impact of changes to their businesses.
4. *Develop their staff.*

With these insights at the forefront, Jordan realized the product-line business model was not serving the value members required. As such, he started sketching design concepts to recommend a member-first overhaul of the entire organization. Soon after, he had a mindset meeting with the board to make sure that the board supported his exploration of an entirely new business model and solidify support and understanding before embarking.

In April 2017, he returned with a prototype business model, digitally transformed in website form, and roughly mapped out using the Wix.com "free website" app. His core thesis was that members wanted to access and play in the sandbox of learn, lead, and connect zones for one price, and the programming HFMA would offer had to align with those goals rather than with the internal structure of various product and service lines.

While the initial model was slightly different from what the team ultimately launched in June 2019, it was enough to get the board's support to go beyond the prototype and to invest resources that allowed the team to do even more design thinking as well as standard research. Ultimately, they digitally transformed the entire business. With that, HFMA members have an open, all-inclusive personalized access to their experience—including all publications, online learning, certifications, and communities. Just like a Netflix experience! There's even a new, strong online community.

The implementation required three simultaneous workstreams. One team worked to refine the business model; another worked on integrating three new technology platforms—association, content, and learning management systems (AMS, CMS, and LMS) into a single system. And the third developed a new, purpose-driven internal organizational structure, organized not around product lines, but about delivering on the four insights with an emphasis on purpose rather than products.

None of this has been easy, but the organization has been happy with its major effort to refocus on its forever promise. Even minor changes have had a major impact on the bottom line—like the recognition that many CFO members wanted their teams to have access to learning. By offering organizational memberships, the team generated $3 million in incremental revenue in the second full year.

Jordan attributes HFMA's success to unqualified support from the CEO and the board, a process that included thousands of hours from longtime members and dozens of staff members, and a big dose of empathy for their ultimate customer.

What to Do to Stay Fresh

You can remedy or altogether avoid these issues by following a few simple guidelines:

1. Ensure that new customer acquisitions outnumber those that leave (acquisition is greater than churn). If you're no longer growing in terms of number of customers, your relevance is shrinking. This is true even if your retention and engagement numbers are high for your existing cohort of members.
2. Invest in onboarding your new members—help them get the most value out of what they're paying for.
3. Look beyond today's happy customers for your "voice of the customer" initiatives. Loyal fans provide the melody, but you need to harmonize with the voices of ex-customers, prospective customers, and prospects that got away.
4. Revisit the mission that launched your business and ask yourself if you'd still execute in the same way. If your goal was transportation, you probably wouldn't use horses anymore, right?

Many organizations have done this well for decades. Universities are often faulted for not catering to the wishes of current students. In fact, they are thinking about changes to align with today's goals *and* tomorrow's as well. Weight Watchers has redefined its core weight loss program multiple times since its founding in 1963. Many gyms offer new classes constantly, swapping out aerobics and Jazzercise for Zumba and TRX.

When you're exclusively focused on longtime members, you may miss the long-term benefits of forever. Growing old with customers might seem natural, but you also must continue to attract and engage with new members. Just because current members aren't looking for alternatives doesn't mean future ones won't, or that the work is done. Bridge the past and future by building a mechanism to hear the concerns of tomorrow's members.

What to Do Next

- Do a quick diagnostic on where your biggest funnel issue is: awareness, acquisition, engagement, or retention. You can look at trends over time. For example, is acquisition declining even as engagement of existing members is strong? Or is acquisition great but churn is on the rise?

- What's the average age of your member? Is that age trending up with your organization? If so, you may have an issue.

> When you're totally focused on longtime members, you may miss the long-term benefits of forever. Growing old with customers might seem natural, but you also must attract and engage with new members.

- Make sure that any "voice of the customer" activities you have consider the voice of lapsed customers and prospects who didn't join. You need multiple voices.

- Take a step back and look at your forever promise with fresh eyes. If you were launching today, and your goal was to deliver on that promise, what kind of a solution would you build?

17 Protect Your Members from Subscription Fatigue

Have you ever felt unwelcome surprise at an annual fee appearing on your credit card, or dismay at the growing list of monthly subscription charges on your statements? If you have, you're not alone. Thirty-six percent of US and UK subscribers find subscriptions frustrating because "it's getting to be expensive to pay for multiple services" according to research by Global Web Index Report.[1] TechCrunch reports that 53 percent of Chinese consumers expect to be using *more* subscription services in two years.[2] And according to a July 2018 report from West Monroe Partners, 84 percent of Americans completely underestimate how much they spend on subscriptions every month.[3] No wonder people around the world are starting to gripe about subscriptions!

Many subscribers complain that they've heard too many pitches to subscribe to the next new thing, when they're not even sure what the value is. They're thinking, "I don't want to subscribe to the software—it's cheaper to just own it outright and I don't need the new features" or "I can't read the issues as fast as they arrive. They're piling up and making me feel guilty." Or even "How many ties-of-the-month does one dad need?" Subscription fatigue is a growing affliction, caused in part by too many choices, confusing pricing, and even manipulative subscription businesses.

> Subscription fatigue is a growing affliction, caused in part by too many choices, confusing pricing, and even manipulative subscription businesses.

How does an organization manage the volume and cadence of its offering in such a way that it's valuable but not overwhelming? You want your members to make your subscription a habit that they won't reconsider, and to trust you enough to stay with you for a long time. Let's look at the various factors contributing to subscription fatigue (and pushback), and how you can avoid contributing to the problem.

Too Many Subscriptions!

Any organization could theoretically become a subscription organization. That's what we've been discussing in this book. You just take a step back and think about the forever goal that drives your members' purchases. Then, brainstorm ongoing benefits you could add and burdens you could remove, repacking the benefits in a way that better creates a forever transaction. So, many organizations have transformed from ownership models to access models and from transactional to relational models. Millennials own less than their parents, subscribing to everything from transportation to entertainment to professional equipment and even food. Consumers and businesses alike love the freedom, flexibility, and security of these relationships. But the number of them is getting out of hand. People struggle to keep track of all the subscriptions.

Deloitte's 13th Digital Media Survey reports that the average streaming video subscriber has three video subscriptions.[4] "With more than 300 over the top video options in the U.S., coupled with multiple subscriptions and payments to track and justify, consumers may be entering a time of 'subscription fatigue,'" said Kevin Westcott, vice chairman, principal, US Telecom, Media & Entertainment lead, Deloitte LLP.

Tracking and managing subscriptions may start feeling like a full-time job, instead of an easy way to solve a problem forever.

In October 2018, banking behemoth Wells Fargo launched Control Tower, enabling customers to cancel subscriptions directly through the bank, without necessarily bothering to cancel with the organizations.[5] Newcomers such as Truebill and Trim are also developing applications to protect consumers against too many subscriptions.

Thomas Smyth, founder and CEO of Trim, compares the relationship between the subscriber and subscription organization as a David and Goliath situation: "As a consumer, you have this whole capitalist society that is constantly getting better at pushing your buttons to get more money out of your pockets. It's a losing battle."[6]

> Millennials own less than their parents, subscribing to everything from transportation to entertainment to professional equipment and even food.

He created Trim, an app that identifies where consumers might be spending too much, and then negotiates on their behalf. Says Smyth, "People say look, it's gotten past the point where I can do this myself. I need a third party, an optimization machine, another business with a corresponding level of sophistication to look at my situation, see where I'm being taken advantage of, and make the problem go away."

Consumers flock to these services to protect themselves from companies who grow their businesses via consumer inertia. Not surprisingly, consumers' trust in, and commitment to, these companies declines. This lack of a trusted relationship is very bad for the world of subscriptions. According to Robert Skrob, author of *Retention Point*, subscriptions are the first thing to go in an economic downturn or a financial setback.[7] As a result of the 2008 financial crisis, more than 40 percent of the subscription businesses Skrob tracked in 2007 were gone by 2009.

To sidestep subscription fatigue, consider bundling multiple benefits under a single subscription. Cable companies have long done this and continue to, even in the "cut-the-cord" era. Apple's new subscription music offering has been bundled with Verizon.[8] This could be good both for Verizon, which gains an additional revenue share and another point of connection with customers, and for Apple, which drives behavior change to their app for music, while expanding its footprint to help it compete with industry-leader Spotify (which has its own bundle deal with video-streaming service Hulu).

Too Many Options and Hard-to-Understand Pricing

Subscription billing is complex. Companies need to bill on a regular schedule, managing automatic payments and the issues that arise when a credit card or bank account no longer works. Price changes can be difficult for an organization to manage, and having multiple tiers of pricing can make things really messy. In December 2019, IDC released an assessment of 13 subscription management platforms, each of which provides myriad ways to bundle and price a subscription's features and benefits. It's possible to create virtually limitless pricing options. You can have multiple tiers, as well as micro-transactions and fixed price options, and different rates by size or industry.

Some software-as-a-service (SaaS) companies literally have a different pricing structure for every client. Why? Because the client asked, and the billing system allows it. It can feel good to give the client exactly what she asks for, even if it creates unnecessary complexity for the SaaS organization or ultimately doesn't give clients what they really need.

Letting your customers dictate the specific features and structures they want is a little like patients self-diagnosing and determining their own prescription. Diagnosis and prescription are your job. The customers are the experts on their pain points, but not necessarily in how to solve their problems. Part of the value you provide is in packaging and combining benefits.

Companies with too many features and incomprehensible billing algorithms can overwhelm subscribers. It's tempting to offer a low introductory price that is eventually raised, but anytime pricing changes, it gives customers a reason to move from membership back to a consumer mindset and to reconsider the initial purchase. To avoid exhausting your subscribers with options, keep your pricing as simple as you can. You can still test pricing plans and terms. It's also perfectly fine, even powerful, to reward your best customers for their loyalty with better pricing or benefits. This approach is the opposite of what most organizations do with low introductory pricing but aligns well with a membership mindset. Experimentation and different options can work, as long as you are transparent with customers. Remember, pricing needs to be simple for the customer to understand—refer to Chapter 12, "Create and Fine-Tune Your Pricing Strategy," for that discussion. The more you tinker with and adjust your pricing on the fly, the less customers will trust you.

Cancellation Woes

Comedian Ryan Hamilton has a whole sketch about how hard it is to cancel a gym membership.[9] Hamilton jokes that the only thing you should need to do to cancel is to say "I want to cancel," but in fact, you often have to cancel in person, or on a particular date, or with a formal letter. These are all tactics to postpone canceling or dissuade it entirely. What irks him is that it can be painfully obvious the customer is not getting the value he's paid for—but it's still hard to get out of the subscription. "As you can see, I've spent $2,600 for four workouts. Now, from where I'm standing, the grounds for cancelation are pretty solid."

> Make sure that your forever promise is powerful enough to justify a forever transaction.

At a 2018 gathering of CEOs using subscription pricing, one proudly explained to me how he'd extended the average revenue per user (ARPU) at his company by an average of two billing payments by requiring subscribers to cancel via phone only and during normal business hours. Needless to say, I was not impressed. Imagine how his customer must feel, having to schedule time to cancel unneeded, unwanted subscriptions! Retaining customers by "hiding the cancel button" is not new. There's a whole world of longtime subscription businesses, known in the trade as "continuity businesses," that bill consumers at the start of each month in exchange for automated product shipments. Think "Book of the Month Club" and those old record clubs that used to give you 12 CDs (or audiocassettes) for one penny if you sign up. They were (in)famous for obstructing cancellation.

Historically, the cable companies have been among the worst offenders. It's notoriously difficult to cancel a cable subscription, and the bills are tough to read and understand. Pricing might start at 60 percent or more off the regular rate, then skyrocket over time. Additionally, because many markets have limited options for consumers, they feel forced to accept whatever they have to pay. With the rise of new streaming content options, consumers now have more choices.

This is why so many apps and financial institutions are providing consumers with ways to fight back. Trim's Smyth explains, "People don't want to cancel, so Trim gathers consumer purchasing power and insights to help it negotiate on the subscriber's behalf. 'I'm negotiating on Robbie's behalf and the right price is . . .' can be highly effective, while saving the consumer time and aggravation."[10]

Investors are starting to understand that increased customer lifetime value doesn't offset the backlash from making it difficult to cancel. Nikhil Basu Trivedi, a managing director at Shasta Ventures, actually sees an upside to easy cancellation policies.[11] "Having a clear cancellation button can lead to a potential save mechanism—you can say 'are you sure?' and offer other choices to the customer (like a different cadence—every other month, or quarterly—or a lower priced plan)—and you can also learn from why a customer is thinking about canceling."

Netflix has always been a leader in giving subscribers freedom to leave. In 2019 when it raised subscription rates, it included the link to cancel in the email announcing the price increase. That's transparency.

Don't hide the cancel button. My experience working with a broad range of companies using subscription pricings has given me confidence that subscribers will often come back if the value is there.

Don't succumb to the temptation to extend a subscription by a month or two, or add features your customers don't need while charging fees you hope they don't notice. These tactics can mean the difference between hitting and missing your quarterly expectations. But any company with a business model predicated on its customers' stupidity or laziness is bound to fail in the long run.

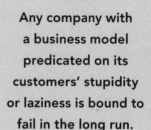

Any company with a business model predicated on its customers' stupidity or laziness is bound to fail in the long run.

And who wants to work at a business like that? If you aim to build forever transactions, based on relationships where customers trust your advice and remain for the long term, don't give them reasons to cancel.

What to Do Next

- Have you optimized your offering with triggers (features that drive sign-up) as well as hooks (features that may be discovered post-transaction that drive loyalty and engagement)?
- Make sure that your service is a "must have" with benefits that become weekly or daily habits. If you have good market share, consider bundling other subscriptions into your offer to deepen the ties.
- Continue to add new features and functionality, ideally without changing your pricing.
- If you were a customer trying to cancel right now, could you find the cancel button? Don't hide it.

18 Going Global with the Forever Transaction

Since publishing *The Membership Economy*, I've been fortunate to have speaking and consulting opportunities across Europe, Asia, Latin America, and Oceania, as well as throughout the United States and Canada. Organizations around the world are pursuing recurring revenue models and the idea of a forever transaction. Examples include American-based global players like Netflix and Amazon, as well as Sweden's Spotify and China's Tencent. Regardless of where they're based, businesses are building long-term, formal relationships with customers across geographies.

Everyone is seeing this trend. The principles of the forever transaction can be applied to great effect almost anywhere. However, you must be sensitive to cultural and legal differences. It may be more efficient for you to deploy your efforts in a few countries where you and your team have a profound understanding rather than spreading your efforts too thinly. Effective tactics for building these relationships can vary by country, as can the legal, shipping, privacy, and cultural environments. Even if your model works great in your home country, when it comes time to expand globally, proceed with caution. This is true whether you're just starting out, leaving your home market for the first time, or adding subscription pricing to your global operations.

A Culture of Global Transparency

When I first started speaking about the Membership Economy, most of my case studies were US-based. Digital innovation was happening in the United States, often in Silicon Valley. Companies based in the United States experimented with membership and subscription pricing domestically first. And, I confess to having cultural myopia. Nearly all of my examples in my first book were US-based, and my knowledge of innovative non-US companies was limited in comparison. No longer. Different cultures, technology footprints, and regulations have created all kinds of really interesting "forever transactions" in every region. I've helped organizations from New Zealand, India, Brazil, China, Sweden, the United Kingdom, Korea, and Colombia to shift their business models and implement deeper, ongoing customer relationships. While the laws and regulations vary, and cultural norms differ by region, it's safe to say that long-term relationships with customers are valuable to organizations around the world. Subscription is a global phenomenon, and no matter what size your organization is today, you should understand how this affects your business.

> Subscription is a global phenomenon, and no matter what size your organization is today, you should understand how this affects your business.

There's no such thing as a "local business" anymore. The instant you have a digital presence, you can be found by people around the world. For example, the South China Morning Post has evolved from a regional (Hong Kong) newspaper mostly for expat business executives to being a global source of Chinese business news. Once, you could only get timely access to SCMP if you were near one of its printing facilities. Now anyone can access its content and become a loyal reader. It's easier than ever to build a global following, or even a global community. You need to decide how to present yourself to global visitors, and whether or not you want them as a part of your market.

Innovation (and the resulting competition) comes from everywhere. In music subscriptions, Apple's biggest competitor comes from the relatively small country of Sweden. Because the Spotify music streaming platform is so popular in the United States, and is listed on the New York Stock Exchange, many don't realize the company has Swedish roots. According to its website, the company has offices in 17 countries including its US headquarters.[1] Spotify has used a freemium strategy, offering listeners a choice of free or premium memberships as a means of getting as many people as possible using the platform. With 191 million monthly active users,[2] Spotify is changing the way the entire world accesses music and challenging Apple's music subscription.

US-based companies face a range of issues when it comes to going global. For example, much has been written about Netflix's pricing decisions in different markets. Every content deal Netflix signs has different regional terms, which means I couldn't download old episodes of *The Good Wife* in Seoul last fall, but I could access a broader range of Korean language titles. Sometimes customers get a significantly better or worse experience by location. For example, many software-as-a-service (SaaS) companies only accept certain currencies, or haven't localized the language inside the apps, even if the website content is in the local language. New offerings come to some markets months or years before they are rolled out to other areas.

Digital communication and social networks mean that everyone, everywhere, can immediately find out who's getting what. This creates lots of challenges for global companies. Loyal customers want to know why they have to wait or why they're paying more. Price-sensitive consumers might try to game the system by pretending to be in a different market to get better deals. Even if you're just starting locally with your forever relationships, assume that customers and prospective customers around the world are aware of your decisions and will notice any inconsistencies. Make sure your logic makes sense and that you communicate clearly. Your decisions are virtually transparent to everyone around the world.

Challenges and Opportunities in Going Global

Before going global, work out the kinks domestically. Georg Richter, CEO of OceanX, the all-in-one direct-to-consumer (DTC) recurring revenue and delivery platform, told me that many startups ask for international shipping when they're launching.[3] He always suggests figuring out the model domestically first, before expanding internationally. The United States is big enough to start.

> Your decisions are virtually transparent to everyone around the world.

Alli Harper heeded this advice when starting with her business OurShelves, a subscription box for diverse children's books.[4] When she launched a pilot in late 2018, her goal was for 50 members to test the operations. She was surprised and delighted to find that with less than three weeks of minimal marketing, her company received more than 300 orders from 40 states for its first box, as well as 22 requests from seven different countries outside the United States. While expanding internationally right away is tempting, Alli knew she needed to systematize US operations before expanding internationally in order to serve all members well. Once OurShelves solidifies domestic operations, it will begin a thoughtful expansion to serve its international audiences.

If you're shipping physical products, you have to handle many issues. According to Richter, your business needs to consider legal situations (think privacy laws in Europe) and retain a global legal team to keep up with ever-changing tax codes. And shipping is always tricky. One time, I ordered a dress on Amazon for a speech I was giving. It took six weeks to arrive from the overseas manufacturer and wouldn't have fit a kindergartner. To Amazon's credit, it refunded my money (it didn't want the dress back), but it illustrates the challenge of guaranteeing regular shipments over long distances, which is exacerbated if you're trying to distribute a product requiring temperature control.

Don't underestimate the complexities of personal data and privacy. The rules vary tremendously and change all the time. Some countries might not allow companies to communicate with customers after they've canceled their subscriptions, while other countries might allow just a single post-cancellation communication. As a result of the broad range of regulatory constraints, something as simple as a "win back" campaign might require literally dozens of variations. Bottom line, make sure you have a great legal team in each market and that you understand the rules in each region.

There are always exceptions, and it might make sense to start with an international footprint. If your organization has a global business already, even if you don't have experience with going direct or offering subscription pricing, you may want to launch globally or do your initial testing in a global market. If you've already figured out how to operate within the laws, regulations, languages, and cultures, it won't be as hard to make the leap, and in some cases, it might be less risky to launch in a smaller or less complex market. If you're based in a country with a limited or nonrepresentative market, success might depend on having operations in several countries from the beginning.

The Challenges of a Complex Operation

Organizations like Netflix, the NBA, and HBO have all offered subscriptions around the world for years. Their offerings go through intermediaries, like cable or satellite providers, as well as through apps that can be accessed directly by consumers without a third party. You can't watch the same sitcoms via Netflix in Colombia as you can in Canada, for example. With the NBA's web of distribution relationships, you generally can't access games with your League Pass subscription in the markets where they're being played. It can be hard for a subscriber to understand why she can't watch her Warriors via the League Pass app on the train ride home from her office in San Francisco.

These organizations deal with the complexity because it allows them to provide value to their global fans and local customers who may be traveling internationally. Working with partners or adjusting strategy for each local market may be an interim step as the organization continues to evolve its offering to deliver consistently on its forever promise. But going global means you might end up with dozens, if not hundreds of unique products, each with its own distribution channel and content array.

It will be challenging to ensure consistent experiences for every customer and to manage pricing. When customers move from market to market, they may get very different experiences and not recognize the offering from place to place. This is the same issue faced by any organization operating globally, but in the Membership Economy, the goal is for the member to relax and trust the organization, which is hard to do when things vary so much. Guthy-Renker, perhaps the most successful of the direct-to-consumer product companies, has launched products ranging from Proactiv skin care line to Wen hair products to Cindy Crawford's Meaningful Beauty. The company used to ship to 75 countries, with seven "local" headquarters, the biggest in Japan. The complexity of global business forced the company to optimize by market, which led to completely different businesses in Asia, Europe, and Australia. Manufacturing and distribution was mostly "local" with many hybrid models. For example, Europe received product from the United States and then distributed from the Netherlands. The variation was complex to manage and not justified by the results. Richter told me he closed most of the international businesses (except Japan) during his tenure at the company.

Forever Is Not Just a US Phenomenon

Around the world, companies are exploring the possibility of building ongoing relationships with their best customers to justify recurring revenue. Your competition—and examples of best practices—may be in other countries. Some of the most sophisticated and successful subscription publications are based in the United Kingdom, including the *Financial Times* and the *Economist*. Understanding your local environment can be key in growth, as the *Financial Times* demonstrated when it dropped its paywall for all Brexit news on Brexit weekend. Not only did it see a huge lift in traffic due to the availability of that free content, it enjoyed a 600 percent spike in digital subscription signups that weekend.[5] Knowing the local market and topics of interest was critical, as was the credibility it had as a leading British publisher. It might have been hard for a US or Asia-based paper to compete with this type of strategy.

Many of the world's most successful music memberships were launched outside the United States. Spotify lists dozens of countries where its service is available, from Algeria to New Zealand. China's Tencent Music offers a similarly broad range of music, but its revenue comes from its karaoke business, WeSing, rather than its streaming service. Investor Fred Liu, managing partner at Hayden Capital, says that's because consumers in Asian markets aren't as willing to pay for content as US consumers.[6] If you're operating outside the United States and interested in building a forever transaction with your customers, you'll want to use the same general practices that I outline in this book. Don't copy any one company, though. Step back, examine the challenges and goals facing your best customers, and ask yourself what you can do to package value in a way that justifies forever.

What to Do Next

- Before expanding beyond your own country's borders, be sure this is the right time, either for competitive reasons or because there's significant demand to justify the investment immediately.
- If you are exploring international expansion, make sure you understand legal, cultural, and competitive challenges as well as the operational challenges. Remember that if you have a different strategy for every country it will be hard to scale—you will need to maintain country expertise in each market.
- Include someone with local insights on the expansion team.

19 Emerging Trends—Forever Is Here Now

When I first started writing about the Membership Economy in 2014, many people didn't get it. They could see how the Membership Economy applied to gyms and Netflix, but not its relevance to *their* business. I spent a lot of time explaining to software-as-a-service (SaaS) businesses that subscription pricing in a vacuum wasn't enough, and to physical product manufacturers that they could benefit from direct, recurring relationships with customers. Today, we're having different discussions. Through thousands of conversations with leaders of organizations, nonprofit and commercial, big and small, in more than 20 industries in a dozen countries over the past several years, I've had a front-row seat to the changes in the Membership Economy. Here are a few trends I'm seeing:

- The expansion from digital to physical goods
- Mature companies learning from startups and adopting the membership model
- The "Amazon Prime" effect: More businesses shifting from simple loyalty programs to premium membership
- Healthcare's slow and painful transition to patient-centered care

- The Membership of Things, or a membership model built on the Internet of Things (IoT)

Each of these trends creates opportunities for disruption. Whether your business is a digital native or a legacy enterprise considering a transition to a customer-focused business with a membership component, a quick tour of these trends should convince you that the time to sit on the sidelines has passed. You have the opportunity to get in front of these changes and use them to your advantage. You certainly cannot ignore them.

Trend 1: The Expansion of Membership from Digital to Physical Goods

A few years ago, most examples of forever transactions came from digital businesses. The rise of new technologies (always-on devices, tools for creating and distributing user-generated content, declining costs of storage, big data analytics, trusted platforms for recurring payments and digital community, to name a few) creates an infrastructure to extend trusted relationships beyond face-to-face.

Today, businesses in the physical world enthusiastically and proactively build forever transactions with the people they serve:

- Consumer packaged goods (CPG) companies offer subscriptions for replenishment (making sure you never run out of your favorite candy, shampoo, or socks) and discovery (subscription boxes). CPG companies also experiment with software-driven services to enhance the product usage, build loyalty, and, in some cases, drive incremental revenue.
- Retailers are getting creative about building value with their customers. Le Tote and Rent the Runway led the way with Netflix-style clothing "rentals." They have been imitated by traditional retailers like Ann Taylor, NY & Co, and Vince.

- Ridesharing services like Uber and Lyft offer memberships for active customers, using different approaches to build deeper loyalty and ultimately to change behavior. Lyft offers a bulk purchase of rides for a fixed monthly subscription, while Uber's Ride Pass is an inexpensive ($15–$25) membership card entitling the member to discounts and no surge pricing.

There are multiple ways for manufacturers and providers of physical experiences like retail, transportation, and hospitality to create ongoing streams of value after the moment of transaction. Many organizations are blending physical and digital benefits to create better experiences for the people they serve. It only takes imagination.

Trend 2: Mature Businesses Are Learning from the Startups

Between 2000 and 2015, venture capital firms poured money into digital natives. Venture money can be patient—many VCs don't expect to sell their shares for seven years or more. With a longer time to reach profitability, entrepreneurs can invest in building strong relationships that pay off over the long term. That gives them a major advantage over public companies against which they often compete. Most public companies have to hit quarterly numbers, even if it hurts their long-term viability.

> There are multiple ways for manufacturers and providers of physical experiences . . . to create ongoing streams of value after the moment of transaction.

Startups aren't the only businesses embracing the forever transaction. Established public businesses are transforming themselves as well. This shouldn't be a surprise, as large companies realize their impermanence. According to a post by Fletcher SCI, only about 25 percent of the top 30 companies in 1988 were still in the top 30 in 2017.[1]

To stay relevant and keep their spots on the Fortune 500 list, companies need to continuously evolve. In light of the attention that subscription-based digital natives like Netflix, LinkedIn, and Salesforce have enjoyed, the boards of many traditional public companies have told their leadership teams to go direct to the customer and build a recurring revenue relationship. More businesses are using customer lifetime value (CLV) as their most important metric. Entire books, like Peter Fader's *Customer Centricity*, have been written about the need for organizations to rethink their structure with customers at the center of everything they do.

> More businesses are using customer lifetime value (CLV) as their most important metric.

Companies that haven't changed fast enough have been left behind.

One of the saddest stories is that of Sears, an early example of the Membership Economy mindset. Since its founding late in the nineteenth century, Sears had been known as a place where Americans could buy anything they needed, regardless of where they lived, with door-to-door delivery. It was like a print version of Amazon. Its mission described its forever promise, explicitly mentioning lasting relationships: "to grow our business by providing quality products and services at great value when and where our customers want them, and by building positive, lasting relationships with our customers."

Sears couldn't compete with Amazon, in part because it didn't evolve to continue to deliver "when and where" customers wanted. Sears filed for bankruptcy protection in October of 2015.[2]

Traditional companies are making the transformation to a forever transaction strategy. Some are changing through acquisition. Unilever bought Dollar Shave Club for $1 billion, and Under Armour bought digital apps MapMyFitness, Endomondo, and MyFitnessPal.

Electronic Arts has added a subscription offering to complement its boxed video game offerings, and Nike incubated EasyKicks, a kids' shoe subscription, and has invested in a Nike membership as part of its commitment to a direct relationship with the people it serves.

Experimentation is happening everywhere—retail, consumer products, airlines, even manufacturing.

Trend 3: Rewards Programs Transition to Premium Membership

Every business has unique attributes that can be incorporated into a model that creates the right kind of forever transaction. Now is the time for all of those quick serve markets, department stores, theme parks, and hotels to step back, articulate their goals and the goals of their best customers, and build a new kind of loyalty model that attracts, engages, and retains those best customers in a mutually beneficial way.

Features of the Amazon Prime model can serve as inspiration, but wholesale copying won't work. Points-based rewards programs are being replaced by premium loyalty memberships. These memberships aim to do more than sell more stuff through discounts and "gifts." Instead, they incorporate better experiences, emotional benefits, and financial incentives. Consumers subscribe to join these premium memberships, paying for access to a higher tier.

Costco is another example of premium loyalty, which predates Amazon Prime and has a stricter model. With few exceptions, you need a membership to shop at Costco. Members pay an annual fee of about $60 and get access to the deals in the store. Some even spend more to be an Executive Member and receive 2 percent back on all Costco purchases, which drives tremendous loyalty. Costco focuses on delivering great value in every product it sells—claiming it doesn't make a profit on product sales. It makes money on membership fees, remaining neutral on the products in the stores. Its forever promise is clear—amazing deals on a range of products from vacations to computers to ketchup to tank tops and diapers. Part of its promise is about value and part of it is discovery—you never know what you're going to find.

Sephora is greatly admired for its multipronged membership strategy. Recently, Sephora introduced a subscription box specifically targeting its subset of customers who love to experiment with the latest products. For $10 a month, Sephora Play subscribers get a box full of samples, access to beauty tips and videos, and in an elegant cross-pollination, Insider Beauty points.

Sephora is a great example of getting out of the "one size fits all" mentality of engagement and personalizing benefits for different kinds of customers.

Other organizations are using paid memberships to deepen relationships with customers who value more than discounts:

- Outdoor apparel and supply company REI charges just $20 for a lifetime membership that goes beyond discounts to include classes and a sense of being an insider.
- Restoration Hardware eliminated coupons outside of its membership program, which costs $100 a year and offers 25 percent savings on full-priced items as well as design and concierge services.
- Six Flags' membership option awards more benefits to guests of its amusement parks who are thinking beyond the current season— lower pricing and greater flexibility after the first year.

The benefits, experiences, and emotional connection to each of these brands differs, but the goal is the same—to build stronger ties and improve customer lifetime value by focusing on the customers likely to get the most value from, and be the most willing to pay for, an ongoing relationship.

Tom Caporaso, CEO of Clarus Commerce, a company specializing in premium loyalty programs, says that companies hold back from embracing this new world out of fear of the unknown and the complexity of subscription pricing.[4] He points out that many companies "have been attached to the discount and promotional strategy for many years and seeing varying levels of success."

This doesn't mean that companies have to completely ditch that program—free and premium can live together. A traditional free loyalty program can still encourage signups and ultimately get customers into the ecosystem. However, when brands incorporate the customized perks and exclusive benefits that a premium program provides, customers truly feel special and valued. It creates deeper, more meaningful connection to the brand, and builds consumer trust over time.

Start with a pilot before jumping in. Consumers will tell you quickly and clearly what they like and don't. Organizations considering this approach, or moving to subscription pricing, have to be okay with failure. Caporaso runs tests all the time, every day, and is quick to note that not every test is a winner. But, he cautions, the world of loyalty programs is changing fast, and "if you're not tinkering and having small failure, you're guaranteed to lose."[5]

> When brands incorporate the customized perks and exclusive benefits . . . customers truly feel special and valued.

Trend 4: Healthcare's Slow and Painful Transition to Patient-Centered Care

The US healthcare system has not been incentivized to deliver care in a patient-centric way.

This is ironic. What forever promise is more meaningful than the promise of health? When is any consumer more vulnerable and sensitive to her experience? Yet much of healthcare has a transactional, product-centric mindset, without aligning the services with the patient's or health plan member's objectives.

Why is this? Historically healthcare is paid for through insurance (including employer-sponsored plans) or the government. The insurance companies regard *employers* who buy health plan products as their primary customers, not the end employee or consumer. Success metrics are mostly around volume and related to reimbursement: hospital days, medical appointments, procedures, and number of people "covered" as members of a plan. Hospital systems view physicians and the payers who reimburse them as their primary customers or necessary partners in their economic model. Value-based care reimbursement models are only now gaining traction—healthcare has been driven by a transactional, "fee for service" model that is still prevalent.

Only the patients, not payers and not providers, have had incentives to stay healthy and out of the doctor's office, operating room, or hospital bed. Year after year, doctors have the same conversations with the same patients: "you should lose weight" . . . "stop smoking" . . . "exercise more" . . . "you're prediabetic". The healthcare system does not make it easy for doctors to invest in preventative care. In fact, in many cases, doctors are compensated for achieving goals (patient visits/day, surgeries/day) which is at odds with preventative care.

> Value-based care reimbursement models are only now gaining traction—healthcare has been driven by a transactional, "fee for service" model that is still prevalent.

It doesn't matter what kind of feel-good language and ads marketing creates—if there aren't financial incentives and metrics tied to patient-centricity, things won't change. Meanwhile, I'd pay a huge premium if I could stay healthy without ever setting foot in a hospital or doctor's office.

Healthcare organizations are slowly moving toward customer-centricity, the idea that their patients are customers and must be treated as such with respect to access, service, price transparency, and so on. Many "consumer-driven" efforts are underway to create greater affinity and "stickiness" between patients and their healthcare providers, often based on an online presence with mobile connectivity.

Sal DeTrane, a digital health venture capitalist in California, states that "progressive healthcare organizations now realize that they are at grave risk of disintermediation if they don't effectively engage and build loyalty with their customers."[6] Health plans must give their "members" a reason to feel affinity for their organization, particularly as members become ever more valuable to them in consumer-oriented plans, such as

Medicare Advantage offerings. Hospitals are building large vertically integrated networks including physicians, hospitals, outpatient facilities, and even their own health plan offerings. These integrated delivery networks (IDNs) require them to build a loyal base of customers that stay within their system for care, enabling them to realize benefits of lifetime customer value. Many drugstores, big box stores, and supermarket chains have opened care centers within their stores and effectively make use of telemedicine models, infringing on clinics and private medical practices. "The traditional healthcare brick-and-mortar model is under assault," according to DeTrane.

Several trends are emerging in the healthcare industry to align the financial interests of healthcare providers with actually maintaining their patients' health. Insurers and healthcare service providers alike are trying to solve the problem. Rich Webb, a healthcare lawyer, arbitrator, and mediator based in New Jersey, points to three trends in particular:[7]

1. Health insurers are creating owned or contracted networks of hospitals and doctors they can offer to their "members," thus blurring the line between healthcare insurance and healthcare services. As an example, Blue Cross and Blue Shield's venture arm's partnership with Sanitas in Texas was announced in April of 2019.[8]

2. Toward a similar goal, hospital and healthcare systems are establishing insurance companies and offering coverage to their patients, a model utilized by Kaiser Permanente for decades. Geisinger Health Plan and Scott & White Health Plan are examples. Entering the insurance business is a difficult trick for healthcare systems given the vagaries of operating a startup insurer under the Affordable Care Act.[9] Hospital systems are also merging to form massive integrated delivery networks providing both insurance plans and services in a unified way. Providence St. Joseph Health and Common Spirit Health (Dignity Health-CHI) are recent examples of this megatrend.

3. Healthcare systems with clinically integrated networks (CINs) are contracting with health insurers and employers to assume financial responsibility for the total cost of healthcare provided to an "attributed" population—in effect, their "membership" of a sort.

Concierge medicine has emerged, particularly in affluent areas, to work around the lack of integrated care in many markets. It can cost consumers $1,200 to $10,000 a year or more to be part of a concierge practice on top of their existing insurance costs, so it's not for everyone. But membership entitles patients to longer appointments, greater access, and a more integrated, personalized health experience.

One Medical, a "members-only technology platform offering an array of concierge medical services," has raised more than $500 million.[10] It aims to provide a concierge-like experience at an affordable price and invites both employers and individuals to participate in its "in network" program.

There is some movement toward an outcomes-oriented approach. As part of the Affordable Care Act, the Centers for Medicare and Medicaid Services (CMS) have adopted a "value-based reimbursement" that incentivizes hospitals based on outcomes rather than procedures.[11]

It seems the federal government is attempting to move its payment model from volume to value. Insurers and employers are following suit and will deploy their own versions of Medicare's tactics.

Reorienting the business processes in a major healthcare system around patient outcomes and true engagement is challenging. Some tested strategies include seeing patients via telemedicine, and compensating physicians by output (patient outcomes) rather than inputs (visits or transactions). Other technical innovation, such as patient engagement solutions and patient-centric data platforms, are being developed as well.

Making this shift and delivering on new member-centric paradigms in healthcare creates risks for everyone. To justify a forever transaction, the entire sector needs to prioritize patient outcomes and engagement as its "mission." That is not the case in US healthcare today. Healthcare providers (hospitals and doctors) remain stuck with one foot in each canoe. They understand and want to participate in the move from volume to value, but the bulk of their compensation remains payable on a volume basis. They operate on fairly thin margins and cannot afford to get too good at providing value (in the form of delivering healthy patients for less money) or they'll put themselves out of business. This will continue unless and until their financial incentives align with those of the patient

A hazy outline in view of a new approach to medicine is emerging, one with a membership mindset and a true forever promise.

and the insurance company. The nascent movement toward greater connectivity between patients and providers must be effectively linked with the hard, cold realities of covered lives and monthly premiums.

A hazy outline in view of a new approach to medicine is emerging, one with a membership mindset and a true forever promise. There are bright spots on the horizon, with interesting experiments among both entrepreneurs and major players. But to scale, they require significant investment, different kinds of partnerships, and, perhaps most of all, cultural change. The timing is good for entrepreneurs and intrapreneurs alike to identify specific pain points and unmet needs facing customers regarding maintaining and optimizing their health. And tech giants like Apple and Google are doubling down on healthcare. How can your organization better deliver on the forever promise of a healthy life?

Trend 5: The Internet of Things (IoT) Enables Membership of Things (MoT)

Running. Tackling. These fundamental athletic activities are getting a boost from an unlikely technology: 3D printing.

You might have seen the commercial for the Adidas Futurecraft 4D shoe. Or maybe you're a sneaker head who actually owns a pair of these

$300 digitally made shoes. With a unique elastomeric lattice cushion, they look cool. More important, the technology paves the way for high-performance shoes customized for each athlete.

If you're a football fan, you may have seen that sentimental 2019 ad about football in America from gear-maker Riddell, which concluded with the importance of protecting athletes and an image of a new kind of helmet. Both the shoes and the helmet feature proprietary, groundbreaking cushioning and energy management systems made on Carbon3D printers.

You can't buy a Carbon3D printer—you can only subscribe. Access to the printers comes wrapped with outstanding customer service and support. Carbon3D CEO Joe DeSimone believes an ownership model would be unethical. "We think of ourselves as concierges to product innovation. Our technology, both for our hardware and the software that runs it, is getting better every day, and we don't want to put our customers in a position of having to wait for the product to be 'finished.'"[12]

Carbon updates the software supporting the printers about every six to eight weeks. It creates modular upgrades to the hardware so existing machines can work seamlessly with new materials, new software, and other, newer printers without being replaced.

Offering a piece of manufacturing equipment as a subscription entails risk. Responsibility for maintenance and obsolescence is on the equipment maker, and there's always the possibility of high churn. But from its launch, Carbon has challenged the standard playbook.

It's not the only company integrating software into physical products that can gather information and insights to provide greater value to the customer.

An April 2019 *Wall Street Journal* article reports "To drum up the new revenue, Caterpillar is connecting machinery to the cloud and alerting miners and builders when they need a tuneup or a new tire . . . [hoping] that monitoring service and the added sales of parts and repairs that it generates will create a steadier revenue stream than sales of new equipment that tend to surge and sink along commodity and building cycles."[13]

Google is betting big on the Membership of Things with its acquisition of Fitbit, the health-tracking wearable, and of Nest, the connected home company famous for its "smart" thermostats, doorbells, and smoke alarms, which collect and analyze data for continuous improvement and safety. And the largest ad company in the world is exploring subscriptions as an alternative method of payment. Consumers can subscribe to video footage collected on their doorbell cameras, for example, or to deeper fitness analytics.

Using sensors and cameras to collect environmental data, manufacturers can provide a huge range of insights and services for their customers, creating new sources of value and recurring revenue streams.

What These Trends Mean for You

While you may be focusing on your direct competitors, they probably won't put you out of business. Disruption is coming from across the globe, or from a company with a totally different business model. It's as if you're running a race and checking behind you for the closest challengers, but other competitors are dropping in from above or outside the track.

Making this shift is important whether you're leading your industry or just starting up, whether you're a car manufacturer or own parking garages, whether you sell flooring or plumbing services. If you don't put the customer at the center of what you do, you will be beaten. It doesn't matter if you're a Bengali news publisher who thinks "Indians

> If you don't put the customer at the center of what you do, you will be beaten.

will never pay for subscriptions" or a British retailer who is sure that "GDPR makes subscription too complex with privacy issues."

As long as customers have choices, organizations must prove they understand their customers' changing needs. We've seen so much change in the past few years as everyone from the smallest sole proprietor to longstanding Fortune 500 companies strives to rebuild their offerings around the ongoing needs of the people they serve. More change is certainly yet to come. The forever transaction is global. It's digital. And customers expect it everywhere.

What to Do Next

- Continue to watch these emerging trends and see if they apply to you.
- Sign up for my email newsletter at www.robbiekellmanbaxter.com to receive continued updates.
- Share your ideas and insights with me at www.robbiekellmanbaxter .com—I'm always learning!

CONCLUSION: HOW TO BUILD AND MAINTAIN A FOREVER TRANSACTION

You made it to the end! You're clearly a person who invests in long-term results—and is willing to put in the work. I'm impressed! Hopefully, you have some deeper insights into how to make this journey to a forever transaction. You know how to start with a forever promise, how to identify and get to know your best customers, and how to build an organization and processes that support recurring revenue. You have the right metrics to track performance and recognize problems before they become insurmountable. You've put your customer at the center of everything you do, remembering that it's about the relationship, not the transaction, and not your exit.

Action items at the end of each chapter can keep you on the right path as you progress. You may find that chapters that don't seem relevant today will become useful tomorrow. If you've applied the principles of this book, you'll be well on your way to making money and achieving your objectives in a predictable, measurable way. You'll be routinely delighting your customers. You also have the opportunity to make a positive contribution to the market, the economy, and the world. I hope your organization, by focusing on the long term, is not only taking care of you and your customers, but also augmenting meaning in your work.

In *The Membership Economy*, I talked about Abraham Maslow's hierarchy of needs. He's the American psychologist who claimed that we all share needs that we try to fulfill, from the most basic to the highest. At the bottom of this hierarchy are your physiological needs (food, shelter, etc.). Once those are met, other needs include risk mitigation, a sense of belonging, esteem, and finally self-actualization, or reaching our full potential. Any good forever promise ultimately ties back to these needs, helping people achieve basic and/or higher order goals.

I encourage you to stay in this place. Operate at the intersection of "what's in it for the customer," "what's in it for us," and "what's in it for everyone else" (Figure 20.1).

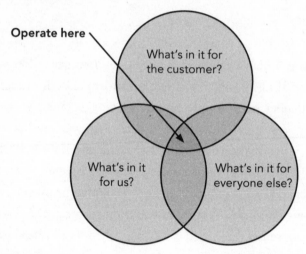

FIGURE 20.1 Operate at the intersection of "what's in it for the customer," "what's in it for us," and "what's in it for everyone else."

Membership is a mindset that the organization has about the people it serves. It's about more than subscription revenue. You can't just jump ahead and design a product without knowing who it's for. And you can't prioritize short-term revenue over the long-term model.

I'm a fan of making money for sure. But I also believe that what I'm doing is in the best interest of my clients. Otherwise I can't do the work. If I didn't consult, I'd be coaching or teaching. (Or I'd own a diner specializing in a good breakfast and a friendly word before people start their days. You can ask my kids. I can make almost any breakfast food, and I'm happy to do it . . . but that's a story for another time.) What gets me out of bed is a sense that I'm helping people be successful at achieving their goals. I hope this book helps you—and I hope you tell me about it (www.robbiekellmanbaxter.com).

When you commit to a forever trans-action, you're focusing on the long term, and you're making intentions transparent to the people involved. It's meaningful work. There's an ethical nature to forever trans-actions. Long-term relationships depend on candor and fit, and also on providing an exit for the ones that don't work out. So congratulations for taking this high road to engagement, loyalty, and, ultimately, recur-ring revenue. Good luck!

> When you commit to a forever transaction, you're focusing on the long term, and you're making intentions transparent to the people involved. It's meaningful work.

GLOSSARY

To help clarify some of the terms in the book, here's a brief glossary.

Acquisition Funnel: Also referred to as conversion funnel or demand funnel, this phrase refers to the customers' journey from the moment of awareness to the moment they become customers. Many organizations use the idea of an acquisition funnel to track how well their marketing activities are working to attract and engage prospects.

Best Customer: Target customer definition based on experience with existing customers. Most desirable customer segment, often a large segment of customers with a high customer lifetime value (CLV).

Business Case Team: Internal small team tasked with developing the detailed argument for investing in membership economy.

Change Management: A discipline devoted to proactively structuring and overseeing the process of transforming an organization, not necessarily in service of a forever transaction. Many professionals call themselves "change management" specialists, some with, some without formal training.

Churn Rate: The percentage of customers who leave (or churn) in a given time period. Note that churn, like interest, compounds over periods. A seemingly low monthly churn rate can be quite high when measured annually.

Customer Lifetime Value (CLV): The net profit of a customer over the customer's entire relationship with an organization.

Engagement: The state of interacting with an organization or its products and services. Engagement metrics can be useful predictors of future customer behavior such as additional purchases or churn.

Evangelists: Customers who feel so strongly about products and services that they freely convince others to try and buy them. Sometimes they are also superusers, but their engagement is targeted around encouraging new members.

Forever Promise: A term coined by the author to mean the commitment made by the organization that justifies a forever transaction. This is similar to a brand promise but is focused on a long-term customer need or desire rather than a product.

Forever Transaction: A term coined by the author to mean a transaction during which the customer makes a decision to continue in a formal relationship with the organization without considering other options in the future—metaphorically removing the customer's "shopper" hat and donning a "membership" hat.

Free Trial: An opportunity for prospects to sample the full benefits of a product or service for a finite period of time without paying. Unlike freemium memberships, free trials last for a finite period.

Freemium: A pricing structure in which members can choose from either a free option that provides ongoing value (forever) or any number of paid subscription options (free + premium = freemium).

Friction: Anything that slows people down when they are trying to engage with the membership or organization. For example, a complicated sign-up process or confusing instructions might cause friction.

Gamification: Applying game thinking and mechanics to nongame settings, usually as a motivator to encourage a certain type of behavior.

Growth Hacking: A term coined by Sean Ellis, founder and CEO of GrowthHackers, to describe a marketing discipline focused specifically on measurable, often low-cost tactics for growth of customers and revenue.

Hourglass Funnel: A specific kind of funnel that tracks a customer's journey from the moment of awareness through the point of becoming a customer, but then continues on, tracking the customer's impact on revenue through referrals and additional purchases.

Loyalty Program: A program designed to drive frequency and depth of purchase, usually in transactional businesses like retail and hospitality, and often using a system of points or punch cards to earn rewards and benefits.

Membership: A program or system that seeks to foster a sense of ongoing belonging in the people it serves.

Membership Economy: A term coined by the author to describe the massive transformational trend in which organizations use a membership mindset to build formal, long-term relationships with the people they serve. Often but not always characterized by tactics such as subscription pricing, use of freemium, and digital community.

Minimum Viable Product (MVP): The simplest version of a product that still achieves the goals of that project. Use of an MVP can be a powerful way to learn from the market without overinvesting. An example often used is if your goal is to create a car, a skateboard might be an MVP, but a tire is not.

Need States: A way of characterizing different customer segments that focuses on customer objectives and priorities rather than demographics or psychographics. Need states can be useful in product definition as well as in creating marketing messages.

Net Promoter System (NPS): A customer-centric approach developed by Fred Reichheld, based on one question: "What is the likelihood that you would recommend Company X to a friend or colleague?" This approach is described in Reichheld's book *The Ultimate Question*. Sometimes people focus just on the points-based calculation of likelihood to promote, known as the Net Promoter Score.

Network Effect: A situation in which each additional member drives value for all existing members just by joining. For example, Skype is more valuable to the hundredth person who joins than the first person. After all, who could that first person Skype with before anyone else joined?

Onboarding: The process of getting a new member fully engaged in the membership. The term is also used to describe the process of acclimating new employees to the organization.

Opt In vs. Opt Out: Some organizations will automatically sign people up for something unless they explicitly say they don't want it, or "opt out." while other organizations require the customer to proactively request to "opt in." Opt in gives more control to the customer.

Over the Top (OTT): Content delivered through the internet as opposed to being delivered through a multiple system operator such as a cable or satellite services. For example, you can access HBO through your cable provider or OTT through HBO Now.

Paywall: An online feature that prevents users from accessing specific options or features without paying a higher price. Paywalls encourage users to upgrade their membership to gain access to greater value.

Pricing Tiers: Different payment options for a subscription service. As the value increases through added features, volume, and service, the subscription rate rises. Most subscription models have multiple pricing tiers.

Product-Market Fit (PMF): A term originally coined by venture capitalist Marc Andreessen as: "being in a good market with a product that can satisfy that market."

Recurring Revenue: Regular payments expected to continue into the future.

Retention Rate: The number of customers who stay over a given time period. Retention is the opposite of churn.

Sharing Economy: Also referred to as the peer-to-peer economy or collaborative consumption, it's a business model that is built around sharing assets. Unlike traditional models, consumers and not the organization maintain ownership of the assets. Examples include Airbnb and Turo.

Software-as-a-Service (SaaS): A software licensing and delivery model in which the vendor licenses software on a subscription basis. The software is centrally hosted in the cloud and customers pay for access, not ownership. Examples are QuickBooks, Salesforce, and Marketo.

Stickiness: Elements of an online experience that encourage the user to stay longer. Critical element in retention.

Subscription: Customers pay a periodic fee for access to services, content, or even physical products. Contrasts with ownership transactions.

Subscription Natives: Businesses that have incorporated subscription pricing since inception.

Superusers: Those especially loyal and engaged members who leverage the power of the community through their participation. Superusers are members who spend a significant amount of time investing in the community.

Switching Costs: The costs incurred by customers when they change from one solution to a substitute.

Transactional Business: Business model in which individually determined payments are made in exchange for specific value with no obligation beyond that single payment.

NOTES

Introduction

1. Blake Droesch, "Which Subscription Services Will US Consumers Sign Up for Next?," eMarketer, May 21, 2019, https://www.emarketer.com/content/which -subscription-services-will-us-consumers-sign-up-for-next?ecid=NL1001.
2. Robbie Kellman Baxter, *The Membership Economy: Find Your Super Users, Master the Forever Transaction, and Build Recurring Revenue* (McGraw-Hill Education, 2015), 1–2.

Chapter 1: Welcome to the World of Forever

1. Michael Henage, "Apple's Biggest Opportunity Could Also Be Its Biggest Problem," Seeking Alpha, June 30, 2019, https://seekingalpha.com/article/4272834 -apples-biggest-opportunity-also-biggest-problem.

Chapter 4: Define Your Forever Promise

1. The Editors of Encyclopaedia Britannica, "Charles Henry Dow," *Encyclopaedia Britannica*, June 24, 2019, https://www.britannica.com/biography/Charles-Henry -Dow.
2. Joe Nocera, "HBO's Anti-Netflix Strategy Is Walking Out the Door," *Bloomberg Opinion*, March 1, 2019, https://www.bloomberg.com/opinion/articles/2019-03 -01/hbo-s-anti-netflix-strategy-was-richard-plepler-now-he-s-leaving.
3. Joe Tenebruso, "Electronic Arts Executives Talk Subscriptions, Esports, and More," The Motley Fool, August 13, 2018, https://www.fool.com/investing/2018 /08/13/electronic-arts-executives-talk-subscriptions-espo.aspx.

Chapter 6: Develop Your First Experiments

1. Michael Blank, multiple interviews with author, Spring 2019.
2. Dan Olsen, *The Lean Product Playbook: How to Innovate with Minimum Viable Products and Rapid Customer Feedback* (Wiley, 2015).
3. "The Business Model Canvas," Strategyzer, accessed June 24, 2019, https://www .strategyzer.com/canvas/business-model-canvas; and "The Value Proposition Canvas," Strategyzer, https://www.strategyzer.com/canvas/value-proposition-canvas.
4. Dan Olsen, email exchange with author, Spring 2019.

Chapter 7: Test, Learn, Adjust

1. Brett Brewer, interview with author, May 20, 2019.
2. FabFitFun, Facebook, March 10, 2019, https://www.facebook.com/pg/FabFitFun /community/.
3. Michael Blank, multiple interviews with author, Spring 2019.
4. Dave Cobban, interview with author, April 15, 2019.

Chapter 8: Manage Emotions, Transform Culture, and Build a Shared Vision

1. J. B. Wood, interview with author, March 19, 2019.
2. Brett Brewer, interview with author, May 20, 2019.
3. Jeanne Bliss, *Would You Do That to Your Mother? The "Make Mom Proud" Standard for How to Treat Your Customers* (Portfolio, 2018).
4. Todd Bishop, "Exclusive: Satya Nadella Reveals Microsoft's New Mission Statement, Sees 'Tough Choices' Ahead," GeekWire, June 25, 2015, https://www.geekwire.com/2015/exclusive-satya-nadella-reveals-microsofts-new-mission-statement-sees-more-tough-choices-ahead/.
5. *Hit Refresh: The Quest to Rediscover Microsoft's Soul and Build a Better World for Everyone* (HarperBusiness, 2017).
6. Brett Brewer, interview with author, May 20, 2019.
7. Often attributed to Peter Drucker, but I haven't seen any evidence thereof.

Chapter 9: Do Acquisitions Make Sense for Your Company?

1. Peter Drucker, *The Age of Discontinuity* (Harper & Row, 1969).
2. Satya Nadella, *Hit Refresh: The Quest to Rediscover Microsoft's Soul and Imagine a Better Future for Everyone* (HarperBusiness, 2017).
3. Larry Dignan, "Under Armour CEO: Connected Fitness Unit Logs $120 million in 2018 Revenue, Brings Consumer Insights," ZDNet, February 13, 2019, https://www.zdnet.com/article/under-armour-ceo-connected-fitness-unit-logs-120-million-in-2018-revenue-brings-consumer-insights/.
4. Peter High, "Under Armour Is Now the Largest Digital Health and Fitness Company on Earth," *Forbes*, September 18, 2017, https://www.forbes.com/sites/peterhigh/2017/09/18/under-armour-is-now-the-largest-digital-health-and-fitness-company-on-earth/#158417205dfc.
5. Laurie Sullivan, "Under Armour Gets Gritness, Furthers Connected Strategy," MediaPost, July 5, 2015, https://www.mediapost.com/publications/article/253284/under-armour-gets-gritness-furhters-connected-str.html.
6. Much of this chapter comes from a series of interviews and email exchanges between author and Michael LaGuardia in May and June 2019.

Chapter 10: Six Common Setbacks and How to Avoid Them

1. "This is Bonnier," Bonnier, accessed June 25, 2019, https://www.bonnier.com/en/page/about-us.

Chapter 11: Choose the Technology to Scale

1. Georg Richter, interview with author, April 23, 2019.
2. Ken Fenyo, "Sizing up the Subscription E-Commerce Market," Fuel x McKinsey, June 13, 2018, https://fuelbymckinsey.com/article/sizing-up-the-subscription-e-commerce-market.
3. "Facebook Changes Its 'Move Fast and Break Things' Motto," Mashable, accessed May 12, 2019, https://mashable.com/2014/04/30/facebooks-new-mantra-move-fast-with-stability/.
4. Nick Statt, "Zuckerberg: 'Move Fast and Break Things' Isn't How Facebook Operates Anymore," c|net, April 30, 2014, https://www.cnet.com/news/zuckerberg-move-fast-and-break-things-isnt-how-we-operate-anymore/.
5. Jane Wilkinson, email exchange with author, May 10, 2019.
6. Kathleen Greenler Sexton, interview with author, March 4, 2019.
7. Michael La Guardia, interview with author, April 12, 2019.

8. Lucinda Southern, "'Long-Term Planning': The Financial Times Now Has 1m Paying Readers," Digiday, April 1, 2019, https://digiday.com/media/long-term -planning-ft-now-1-million-paying-readers/.
9. Scott Brinker, "Marketing Technology Landscape Supergraphic (2019): Martech 5000 (actually 7,040)," Chiefmartec.com, April 4, 2019, https://chiefmartec.com /2019/04/marketing-technology-landscape-supergraphic-2019.
10. Kim Terry, email exchange with author, May 8, 2019.
11. Eric Okerstrom, email exchange with author, June 3, 2019.

Chapter 12: Create and Fine-Tune Your Pricing Strategy
1. "What Do Airline Customers Really Want?," Boxever, April 17, 2019, https://www .boxever.com/airline-consumer-survey/.
2. Robbie Kellman Baxter, *The Membership Economy: Find Your Super Users, Master the Forever Transaction, and Build Recurring Revenue* (McGraw-Hill Education, 2015), 73–76.
3. Richard Reisman, *FairPay: Adaptively Win-Win Customer Relationships* (Business Expert Press, 2017). https://www.fairpayzone.com/p/fairpaybook.html
4. Lucinda Southern, "'Long-Term Planning': The Financial Times Now Has 1m Paying Readers," Digiday, April 1, 2019, https://digiday.com/media/long-term -planning-ft-now-1-million-paying-readers/.

Chapter 13: Essential Metrics for Long-Term Relationships
1. Jamie Powell, "The Quality of Quantity at Netflix," *Financial Times*, October 19, 2018, https://ftalphaville.ft.com/2018/10/19/1539949288000/The-quality-of -quantity-at-Netflix/.
2. Fred Reichheld, *The Ultimate Question: Driving Good Profits and True Growth* (Harvard Business School Press, 2006), https://www.amazon.com/Ultimate-Question -Driving-Profits-Growth/dp/1591397839.

Chapter 14: Forever Is a Long Time: Don't Take Shortcuts
1. DHH (@dhh), Tweet, February 18, 2019, https://twitter.com/dhh/status /1097645910719266816?s=21.
2. "Kate Hudson's Activewear Subscription Service Faces Backlash," CBS This Morning, October 6, 2015, https://www.cbsnews.com/news/kate-hudson-fabletics -subscription-service-vip-faces-backlash-customers-complain/.
3. Tony Chen, Ken Fenyo, Sylvia Yang, and Jessica Zhang, "Thinking Inside the Subscription Box: New Research on E-commerce Consumers," McKinsey & Company, February 2018, https://www.mckinsey.com/industries/high-tech/our-insights /thinking-inside-the-subscription-box-new-research-on-ecommerce-consumers #0, pulled 3/25.
4. Zuora, The Subscription Economy Index™, March 2019, http://info.zuora.com/rs /602-QGZ-447/images/subscription-economy-index-q4-2018.pdf.
5. "Apple Special Event. March 25, 2019. From the Steve Jobs Theatre," https://www .apple.com/apple-events/march-2019/.
6. Todd Spangler, "MoviePass Has Lost Over 90% of Its Subscribers in Less Than a Year (Report)," *Variety*, April 18, 2019, https://variety.com/2019/digital/news /moviepass-subscribers-loss-crater-225000-1203192468/.
7. Josh Barro, "SoulCycle Has Found a Brilliant Way to Monetize Loyalty," Intelligencer, June 9, 2019, http://nymag.com/intelligencer/2019/06/soulcycle-has-found -a-brilliant-way-to-monetize-loyalty.html.
8. Kim Stone, interview with author, February 22, 2019.

9. Scott Ostler, "Warriors' New Arena Gives Some Season-Ticket Holders Sticker Shock," *San Francisco Chronicle*, March 1, 2018, https://www.sfchronicle.com/sports/ostler/article/Warriors-new-arena-gives-some-season-12720962.php.

Chapter 15: Continue to Iterate

1. Local Government Commission, accessed March 8, 2019, https://www.lgc.org/resources/community-design/lpu/feb2016/.
2. Robbie Kellman Baxter, *The Membership Economy: Find Your Super Users, Master the Forever Transaction, and Build Recurring Revenue* (McGraw-Hill Education, 2015), 202.
3. Jonathan Hsu, interview with author, May 1, 2019.
4. Tren Griffin, "12 Things About Product-Market Fit," May 2, 2019, https://a16z.c7m/2017/02/18/12-things-about-product-market-fit/.
5. Andy Rachleff is quoted in many articles on this topic, including this one on the blog of venture capital firm Andreessen Horowitz: https://a16z.com/2017/02/18/12-things-about-product-market-fit/.
6. Jonathan Hsu, "A Quantitative Approach to Product Market Fit," June 5, 2019, https://tribecap.co/a-quantitative-approach-to-product-market-fit/.
7. Dawn Sweeney, conversations with author, Fall 2015.

Chapter 16: Stay Forever Young: Avoid Aging with Your Members

1. Pål Nedregotten, email exchange with author, June 1, 2019.
2. Robert Skrob, email exchange with author, June 16, 2019.
3. 2017–2018 HFMA Annual Report, https://www.hfma.org/content/dam/hfma/Documents/PDFs/HFMA%20Annual%20Report%202017-18.pdf.
4. Garth Jordan, interview with author, June 7, 2019.

Chapter 17: Protect Your Members from Subscription Fatigue

1. Global Web Index Report, "The Entertainment Trends to Watch in 2019," https://blog.globalwebindex.com/trends/entertainment-trends-2019.
2. Sarah Perez, "Subscription Fatigue Hasn't Hit Yet," TechCrunch, May 22, 2019, https://techcrunch.com/2019/05/22/subscription-fatigue-hasnt-hit-yet/.
3. Joanna Stern, "Stop Wasting Money on Unnecessary Monthly Subscriptions," *Wall Street Journal*, May 9, 2019.
4. "Digital Media Trends Survey, 13th Edition—A Snapshot of Consumer Media Consumption," Deloitte Insights, https://www2.deloitte.com/insights/us/en/industry/technology/digital-media-trends-consumption-habits-survey.html?id=us:2el:3pr:4di5116:5awa:6di:MMDDYY:&pkid=1006161.
5. "Wells Fargo Launches Control Tower^SM, New Digital Experience for Customers Nationwide," Business Wire, October 1, 2018, https://www.businesswire.com/news/home/20181001005683/en/Wells-Fargo-Launches-Control-Tower-SM-New.
6. Thomas Smyth, interview with author, April 30, 2019.
7. Robert Skrob, email exchange with author, June 9, 2019.
8. Todd Spangle, "Verizon Bundles Apple Music with Top-Tier Unlimited Wireless Plans for No Extra Charge," *Variety*, January 15, 2019, https://variety.com/2019/digital/news/verizon-apple-music-free-unlimited-plans-1203109494/.
9. Ryan Hamilton—Canceling a Gym Membership, Economics Media Library, accessed June 25, 2019, https://econ.video/2017/12/19/ryan-hamilton-canceling-a-gym-membership/.
10. Thomas Smyth, interview with author, April 30, 2019.
11. Nikhil Basu Trivedi, email exchange with author, May 14, 2019.

Chapter 18: Going Global with the Forever Transaction

1. Spotify, accessed January 29, 2019, https://www.spotify.com/us/about-us/contact/.
2. Spotify, Q3 2018 report.
3. Georg Richter, email exchange with author, May 5, 2019.
4. Alli Harper, email exchange with author, Spring 2019.
5. Jessica Davies, "How the FT Drove Digital Subscriptions Sales by 600 Percent over Brexit Weekend," Digiday, June 29, 2016, https://digiday.com/uk/ft-drove-digital-subscriptions-sales-600-percent-brexit-weekend/.
6. Fred Liu, interview with author, April 30, 2019.

Chapter 19: Emerging Trends—Forever Is Here Now

1. Holly McClelland, "Past and Present: The Fortune 500 in 1988 vs. 2018," Fletcher/CSI, accessed January 31, 2019, https://fletchercsi.com/strategy/past-and-present-the-fortune-500-in-1988-vs-2018/.
2. Jeremy Bowman, "Sears' Bankruptcy: How It Got Here—and What Happens Next," The Motley Fool, October 15, 2018, https://www.fool.com/investing/2018/10/15/sears-bankruptcy-how-it-got-here-and-what-happens.aspx.
3. Jordan Weissmann, "Amazon Is Jacking up the Cost of Prime, and It's Still Cheap," Slate, March 13, 2014, https://slate.com/business/2014/03/amazon-prime-price-increase-it-s-still-inexpensive.html.
4. Mike Mish Shedlock, "Amazon Prime Subscribers Hits 100 Million: $10 Billion in Annual Prime Revenue," Mish Talk, April 19, 2019, https://moneymaven.io/mishtalk/economics/amazon-prime-subscribers-hits-100-million-10-billion-in-annual-prime-revenue-ysVLXhOPTkO2cvO3sOvOkw/.
5. Amit Sharma, "How These 3 Brands Are Taking Loyalty Beyond Points," Adweek, April 25, 2018, https://www.adweek.com/digital/how-these-3-brands-are-taking-loyalty-beyond-points/.
6. Tom Caporaso, interview with author, May 9, 2019.
7. Rich Webb, email exchange with author, April and May, 2019.
8. Bruce Japsen, "Big Blue Cross Plans to Open Primary Care Clinics in Texas and Beyond," Forbes, April 8, 2019, https://www.forbes.com/sites/brucejapsen/2019/04/08/big-blue-cross-plans-to-open-primary-care-clinics-in-texas-and-beyond/#59726d562921.
9. Rich Webb, email exchange with author, April and May, 2019.
10. Bruce Japsen, "Big Blue Cross Plans to Open Primary Care Clinics in Texas and Beyond," Forbes, April 8, 2019, https://www.forbes.com/sites/brucejapsen/2019/04/08/big-blue-cross-plans-to-open-primary-care-clinics-in-texas-and-beyond/#59726d562921.
11. Sarah Maslin Nir, "New York's Largest Hospital System Is Closing Its Insurance Business," New York Times, August 24, 2017, https://www.nytimes.com/2017/08/24/nyregion/northwell-health-insurance.html.
12. Crunchbase, accessed March 25, 2019, https://www.crunchbase.com/organization/one-medical-group#section-overview.
13. "CMS Hospital Value-Based Purchasing Program Results for Fiscal Year 2019," CMS.Gov, December 3, 2018, https://www.cms.gov/newsroom/fact-sheets/cms-hospital-value-based-purchasing-program-results-fiscal-year-2019.
14. Joe DeSimone, interview with author, March 8, 2019.
15. Austen Hufford, "Caterpillar Digs for New Services Revenue," Wall Street Journal, April 8, 2019, https://www.wsj.com/articles/caterpillar-digs-for-new-services-revenue-11554724802.

ACKNOWLEDGMENTS

To find success in a forever transaction or organization, you'll need a team of people all dedicated to serving the member or customer and fulfilling the forever promise. The same thing is true of writing a book like this. In my attempt to deliver on the promise of this book, I've called on a team of people—industry experts, clients, practitioners, editors, friends, and mentors. Their contributions have been critical to the end result. These are some of the members of my "Forever" team:

I was smart enough this time to bring in editorial big guns from the very beginning. Anne Janzer is both an expert on Subscription Marketing (check out her book of that name) and an expert on writing who has written multiple books on that topic. She has been my thought partner throughout this process, and her fingerprints are everywhere.

Heather Hunt did two (or was it three) complete read-throughs of the manuscript in record time, cutting deadwood, asking tough questions, and clarifying confusing passages. And she did it while on a family road trip across the west. Thank you to Cindy Orshonsky, who once again created graphics and formatted the book for clarity and consistency.

I interviewed more than 20 thought leaders and practitioners including Alli Harper, Anthony Napolitano, Dan McCarthy, Dave Cobban, Eric Kurt, Eric Okerstrom, Fred Liu, Garth Jordan, Georg Richter, Jason Rosenthal, Joe DeSimone, Jonathan Hsu, Kim Terry, Kim Stone, Lisa Farrow, Mike Blank, Michael La Guardia, Nancy Flowers, Nikhil Basu Trivedi, Pål Nedregotten, Raghu Iyengar, Richard Kestenbaum, Richard Reisman, Sal DeTrane, and Sandeep Parekh. Their experiences are the heart of the content, and what makes this book special. So many practitioners and thought leaders have shared their challenges and "aha" moments with me, and it has enabled me to share a real view from the trenches.

I invited a lot of people to read my book before I sent it off to the publisher. I wanted to get the perspective of entrepreneurs and executives, but also avid business book readers not necessarily interested in this topic, and fellow authors to push me on structure and style. Thank you to all the people who spent hours (and hours) this hot summer, and into the rainy fall, reading my pages: Alli Harper, Bob Shullman, Brennan Pursell, Camille Landau, Caroline Osinski, Cristi Jakubik, Dan Olsen, Dan Siegel, Det Ansinn, Felix van der Sommen, Godfrey Nazareth, Guillermina Castellanos, Jana Danielson, Jane Wilkinson, Joan Lambert, Joe Tatum, Julian Thorne, Karen Cassel, Leslie Crutchfield, Lisa Farrow, Liza Hanks, Mark Vinson, Mary Byers, Mihaela Akers, Naotake Murayama, Paul Shepherd, Rebecca Bloom, Rich Webb, Robert Kviby, Robert Skrob, Sal DeTrane, Sasha Norkin, Sharon Richmond, Steve Kelly, and Ted Bongiovanni.

I am thrilled to be working with the same publishing team as I did for *The Membership Economy*, led by Donya Dickerson at McGraw-Hill including Jeff Weeks, Nora Hennick, Amanda Muller, and Scott Kurtz. Thank you to my agent, Ted Weinstein, who pushes to make things better in all ways.

I'm grateful to all of my clients. They've shared their journeys with candor, bumps, and all. They have worked with me to expand my ideas, develop and test frameworks and get those ideas and frameworks onto paper. I have enjoyed and learned from every single one of them. How many people in client services can say that?

My family, the many Kellmans, Agustins, and Baxters, have been patient and generous with me, as they always are. My mom, dad, sister and husband carefully read each page, looking for confusing passages, repetition and inappropriate comma usage. I come from a family of readers and writers, but even more, a family where support is always explicit as well as implicit. My extended family gives me space and encouragement, always. I'm lucky, on the other side of 50, to still have the support of my vibrant and doting parents, who have truly supported all my big decisions, which has given me so much confidence. My relatives through marriage—my husband's family and my sister's—are close friends and trusted advisors who picked up the slack when I was deep into writing or editing.

Most of all I am most grateful to my immediate family. To my three intelligent, independent, and loving children, Molly, Annabel, and Nate, who still think I'm a "cool mom" even though I'm often preoccupied with work and writing. And to Bob for keeping the pressure of the rest of the world from slowing me down.

INDEX

Page numbers followed by *f* and *t* refer to figures and tables, respectively.

ABOUT THE AUTHOR

Robbie Kellman Baxter is the founder of Peninsula Strategies LLC, a consulting firm that helps companies excel in the Membership Economy and a subject matter expert on membership models and subscription pricing. Her first book, *The Membership Economy: Find Your Superusers, Master the Forever Transaction, and Build Recurring Revenue*, is an international bestseller. Her clients have included Microsoft, the *Wall Street Journal*, and Electronic Arts. Over the course of her career, Robbie has worked in or consulted to clients in more than 20 industries.

As a public speaker, Robbie has presented to thousands of people in corporations, associations, and universities. Robbie has been quoted in or written articles for major media outlets, including *Harvard Business Review*, the *New York Times*, *CIO Magazine*, *Brand Quarterly*, *Leader to Leader*, *Harvard Business Review*, and the *Wall Street Journal*. She has an AB from Harvard College and an MBA from the Stanford Graduate School of Business.

> **To learn more, or get in touch with Robbie,**
> **visit www.robbiekellmanbaxter.com.**

The definitive book on why subscriptions are taking over and what it means for you.

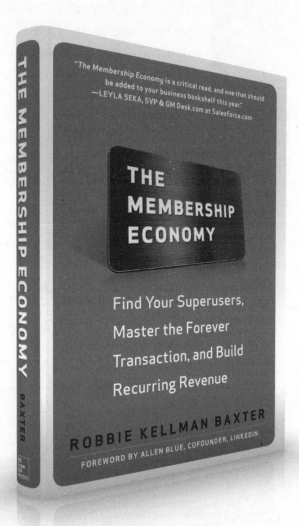

"The Membership Economy is a critical read, and one that should be added to your business bookshelf this year."
—LEYLA SEKA, SVP & GM Desk.com at Salesforce.com

THE MEMBERSHIP ECONOMY

Find Your Superusers, Master the Forever Transaction, and Build Recurring Revenue

ROBBIE KELLMAN BAXTER

FOREWORD BY ALLEN BLUE, COFOUNDER, LINKEDIN

978-0071839327